# BEN FRANKLIN'S PRIVATEERS

*Attributed to Jean Baptiste Greuze*

DR. BENJAMIN FRANKLIN

# Ben Franklin's Privateers

## A Naval Epic
## of the American Revolution

*By*

## WILLIAM BELL CLARK

LOUISIANA STATE UNIVERSITY PRESS

*Baton Rouge*

OTHER BOOKS BY WILLIAM BELL CLARK:

*The First Saratoga* (1953)
*Captain Dauntless, the Story of Nicholas Biddle of the Continental Navy*
 (1949)
*Gallant John Barry, Naval Hero* (1938)
*Lambert Wickes, Sea Raider and Diplomat* (1932)
*When the U-Boats Came to America* (1929)

MANUFACTURED IN THE UNITED STATES OF AMERICA

BY THE COLONIAL PRESS INC., CLINTON, MASSACHUSETTS

# *Preface*

Many fascinating tales have been told about Benjamin Frankin. And despite so-called definitive biographies many more await the telling. This is expressly true of his involvement in maritime matters. His concern in naval activities in European seas, other than with the exploits of John Paul Jones, has been largely ignored. Granting American commissions to French-owned and Irish smuggler-manned privateers is a case in point. The purpose has been misunderstood and slighted by those who have touched upon the subject. Yet it provides an illuminating picture of one of Franklin's greatest objectives during the war years—the liberation of American prisoners in England.

While he might write to Congress that, "we continue to insult the Coasts of the *Lords of the Ocean* with our little Cruisers," his reward was not the prizes they brought in. He had no investment in the privateers and hence no prospect of financial gain by the capture of enemy shipping. His interest lay primarily in the prisoners they took who could redeem "our poor Countrymen." For that reason and that alone, he issued commissions authorizing the cutters *Black Prince, Black Princess,* and *Fearnot* to foray against British sea trade. "The Prisoners to exchange for Americans," he wrote, "are all the Advantage I have for my trouble."

This trouble and the sensational cruises his privateers

made combine to form this epic. Some new figures are introduced into American naval history: Stephen Marchant, gullible Boston shipmaster, who found himself a figurehead; Luke Ryan, polished Irish smuggler, the daring leader of the enterprise; Patrick Dowlin, another Irishman, who succeeded Marchant in command of the *Black Prince;* Edward Macatter, a third lad from the Old Sod, who commanded the *Black Princess;* John Torris, voluble French owner of the privateers; Francis Coffyn, Flemish-born agent for the United States at Dunkirk; William Hodgson, London merchant, who negotiated prisoner exchanges; David Hartley, British member of Parliament in the guise of a good Samaritan; and a number of minor characters.

Primarily, however, this is a story of Benjamin Franklin as a much-harassed Minister Plenipotentiary, a persistent humanitarian, an unwilling judge of the admiralty, and a frequently exasperated gentleman, who voiced his dislike of all his roles with the flat statement: "I am heartily tired of Ships and Cruises."

I am greatly indebted to Dr. William E. Lingelback, Librarian, and Mrs. Gertrude D. Hess, Assistant Librarian, and her obliging assistant, Mrs. Ruth A. Duncan, of the American Philosophical Society, for assistance in locating letters and documents and for placing at my disposal the Society's vast storehouse of Frankliniana. Similar courtesy and consideration were extended by Mr. J. Harcourt Givens, in charge of the Manuscript Division of the Historical Society of Pennsylvania, and his assistant, Miss Catharine H. Miller. My appreciation goes also to Mr. Walter Yust, editor, and his associates in the research service of *Encyclopædia Britannica,* who ferreted out for me the location of long-forgotten hamlets on the coasts of England, Scotland, Ireland, and Wales. I wish also to express my deep gratitude to Mr. Arthur J. Sussel of Philadelphia, for permission to use for the first time the rare portrait of Benjamin Franklin, and to Miss Adele Drouet, of Newcomb College, New Orleans, who translated a number of French letters regarding the privateers.

All of the illustrations in this book, with the exception of the frontispiece and one other, are of documents in the Franklin Papers, APS, and are used through the courtesy of the American Philosophical Society. The copy of Franklin's commission to Marchant is reproduced through the courtesy of the Admiralty Papers, Public Records Office, London.

WILLIAM BELL CLARK

*Brevard, North Carolina*

# Contents

# Illustrations

# Maps

# BEN FRANKLIN'S PRIVATEERS

# Prologue

Black as the darkness enshrouding her, the smuggling cutter *Friendship*, lean, long, and rakish, lay moored in Poolbeg. Her late crew, some dozen desperate characters from the town of Rush, had been lodged the previous afternoon in the Black Dog. Come daylight the cargo of French brandy and Dutch tea would be landed, confiscated and stored in His Majesty's customhouse. Nine officers of the revenue service had remained on board; a safeguard against Dublin's water-front denizens, whose Irish thirst and thieving instincts might otherwise be too sorely tempted. Such show of force would be ample deterrent to prowlers from the wharves and docks of the river Liffey.

There could be no peril from elsewhere. Ever since the French king, in the previous summer of 1778, had avowed intentions to "make reprisals and act hostilely against England," Dublin had been strengthening harbor defenses. By fall two floating batteries at the entrance to Poolbeg mounted so many heavy guns that shipping was considered secure against enemy forays. Hence, only a two-man watch had been posted fore and aft upon the cutter that early spring night. The other seven of His Majesty's servants of the revenue service had retired; the petty officer commanding to the master's cabin aft; the others below to the bunks and hammocks of the dispossessed crew.

A gray mist hung above the water, dimming the feeble street lamps which marked where Dublin slept, and concealing the surface of Poolbeg save for the thin paths reflected by the cutter's riding lights. The night was as silent as it was dark, the air heavy. In the bow and astern on the quarter-deck the watch drowsed. Neither man heard the faint creak of muffled oars upon thole-pins. Neither noted two approaching shadows, blacker than the surrounding darkness and concealing the crew supposed to be behind iron bars in Dublin's jail.

When, belatedly, they sensed danger both boats had run alongside—one at the gangway ladder and the other at the forward end of the port channels—and the smugglers, heavily armed, were over the bulwarks and upon them. No time then to give alarm or even snap a pistol. Shouts for their slumbering comrades were stifled by blows from pistol stocks, stunning both men. The petty officer in the stern cabin, befuddled by sleep, was overpowered, bound and gagged. The bewildered ones below were called up the companionway ladder, one at a time, relieved of their weapons and neatly trussed. Not a shot had been fired; not a voice raised to a pitch which might have alarmed the shore. But the cutter still lay within hailing distance of the customhouse, and darkness had begun to lift.

Orders were given in whispers and obeyed with alacrity by men who realized that the lawless act of that night would put a price upon their heads. The cable was slashed, losing an anchor, but avoiding the telltale creak of the capstan. A faint breeze had begun to blow out of the west, and the tide was ebbing. As Dublin's lights slowly receded, the first piece of canvas was let out. By the time the black-sided cutter had crossed Poolbeg all sail was set. She slipped without challenge between the floating batteries at the harbor mouth, whose garrisons looked only seaward for trouble. Shortly thereafter the officers of His

Majesty's revenue service were unbound and, with their wounded companions, placed in one of the boats. Dawn broke as the disgruntled servants of George III pulled away for the distant shore. The wind strengthened and the cutter, clearing Dublin Bay, veered northward around Howth, headed for the coastal waters off Rush.[1]

Eighteen men comprised the band on board the *Friendship*. Most of them were members of her crew. The others had slipped into Dublin, passed word to the prisoners that arms awaited them, and, quite likely, assisted in the break from the Black Dog. Their leaders were the first and second mates of the cutter, Edward Macatter and Alexander Weldin, each with aliases to puzzle and bedevil the revenue officers. Macatter, in particular, was known variously as Richard Bennett and Captain Wilde. Among the others on board were Patrick Dowlin, Thomas Connor, Bartholomew Mulvaney, Michael Morgan, Bryan Rooney, Edward Duff and Timothy, John and Christopher Kelly—the likes of them noted as smugglers all along the coasts of Ireland, Wales, and Cornwall.[2]

Instigator of the daring exploit was none of these. He was the owner and master of the cutter, a remarkable young Irishman named Luke Ryan. By lucky chance he had been ashore when His Majesty's revenue officers had

[1] Numerous fragmentary accounts of the daring cutting out of the smuggling cutter appeared in the newspapers and in contemporary letters. Interest in the exploit continued for several years, and, as late as August 22, 1780, the London *Chronicle* was recording the arrest at Dublin of one Rourke, who "appears to be one of the party concerned in cutting the Black Prince out of Poolbeg, and wounding some of Mr. Draper's men, who had the vessel under seizure." That the cutter originally was called the *Friendship* was not disclosed until ten years later, in an account in the *Pennsylvania Journal*, Philadelphia, October 7, 1789.

[2] Identity of the smugglers was divulged in an affidavit by Robert Rositer, mariner, before two justices of the peace at Swansea, Wales, and enclosed by them on July 22, 1779, to the Secretary of the Admiralty, where it was filed along with other "Letters from Sundrys giving inform$^n$ of the piratical Vessel Black Prince."

seized her. Thereafter he had planned both jail delivery and cutting-out enterprise, and had supplied arms and reinforcements. Then he had ridden hard for Rush, that haven of the smuggling brotherhood some twenty miles to the northward, to recruit more hands.

By midmorning the *Friendship* was past Lambey Island, standing towards shore. Macatter hailed an inbound fishing boat and sent word of their arrival. When Ryan came off, the crew lined the rail to greet him with Irish exuberance and to welcome as vociferously eighteen Rushmen he brought with him. He stepped on board, small of stature, slight of build, and meticulously groomed; a fastidious and handsome young gentleman whose appearance bordered upon effeminacy.

This twenty-five year old mariner, however, belied his looks. He claimed to have been born in France, son of a captain in Dillon's Irish regiment in the service of His Christian Majesty, a pretension which had given him great aplomb. Actually, he was the only child of Michael and Mary Ryan, of Kenmure, a hamlet some thirteen miles from Dublin, where the senior Ryan was a humble farmer. Educated in a country school at Hackettstown, and bound to a ship carpenter in Skerries, young Luke had taken to smuggling rather than boatbuilding the moment his apprenticeship had ended. In this hazardous pursuit he demonstrated a mind keen in outwitting the law, a character for audacity in landing cargo, a reputation for courage, and a natural capacity as a leader. With intuitive knowledge of seamanship, he had commanded a smuggling wherry of his own before reaching his majority. By the spring of 1779, he had become the anathema of His Majesty's revenue officers from Belfast around to Dover.[3]

[3] Luke Ryan was taken in the French privateer *Le Cologne,* on April 17, 1781, and tried for piracy a year later. During his trial and his nu-

As the alarm undoubtedly would have been sounded and revenue sloops and cutters would be out in pursuit, Ryan ordered the bow pointed southeastward, running for Cardigan Bay on the Welsh coast. His intent was to land the liquors and tea at some uninhabited spot on the shore between Barmouth and Cardigan. Revenue vessels to the contrary, he wanted to realize upon the goods which so narrowly had escaped the King's customhouse at Dublin. Smugglers well conceal their hideouts, so who could know where Luke disposed of his cargo? With it, however, went ashore one of his hands, who had no stomach for further adventure.[4]

Once the goods were landed and carted off, Ryan disclosed his plan. No longer would the British regard them as smugglers who, if captured, would be given short prison terms, and whose vessel and cargo might be confiscated. Retaking the cutter from the royal collector of the revenue, along with wounding several of his officers, was a crime punishable by death. They were now—every man on board—pirates in the eyes of all Englishmen. If caught, they would have short shrift and soon grace gibbets at Plymouth, Portsmouth, or Sheerness. To avert this fate, Luke proposed proceeding for Dunkirk and offering the *Friendship* to some merchant as a privateer. Perhaps a commission could be secured from the Americans. They

merous prior appearances before various magistrates much was disclosed of his antecedents, pretensions, and appearance. "The Person of Luke Ryan is by no means of the athletic frame, which the Character he has sustained seems to require," ran one description of him in the *Public Advertiser*, London, October 16, 1781. "He is of small stature, rather approaching Effemincy, his Countenance is Pale and Sickly, but marked with the strongest Sensibility, and his Address is perfectly that of a Gentleman."

4 The smuggler with a change of heart was one Bowen, who was apprehended in Dublin in April, 1780, and who confessed "that he was employed by Ryan . . . but added that he did not remain on board the Black Prince afterwards longer than a few days, having prevailed on the rest to set him ashore in Wales." Despite his refusal to stick with the smugglers, Bowen, according to the London *Chronicle* of April 11–13, 1780, was committed for piracy.

could all swear allegiance to the United States; then as American subjects they might be immune, if taken, from criminal prosecution and be regarded as prisoners of war. It was a heartening proposition. With inherent hatred for the British, the men scented prizes and profits and responded with enthusiasm.[5]

So, it was up sail and southward, out through St. George's Channel and around Land's End. In the English Channel the weather turned stormy with strong west winds. One hard gale carried away the boom, but alert seamanship prevented worse disaster. Once into the narrow Strait of Dover, Ryan hugged the French shore, close in past Calais and on until the tall tower of Dunkirk loomed in the dawning of a day some two weeks after departure from Poolbeg.[6]

[5] That Ryan did not exaggerate the peril in which he and his crew stood finds confirmation from an Englishman, who advised the British Admiralty that the smuggling craft "seems to be a Pirate and if we are rightly informed was run away with from dublin River and is maned with Several Fellows that broke out of Dublin Gaol and there fore are a desperate Crew having the Halter about their Necks." This letter shared the fate of many others sent to the Admiralty; it was filed without action.

[6] A circumstantial account of the cutting-out enterprise, and the subsequent arrival at Dunkirk, even to the boom carried away in the English Channel, is contained in a letter, dated June 24, 1779, which a gentleman sent to the London *Chronicle*, where it was published in the issue of July 3–6, 1779.

## CHAPTER I

# Dr. Franklin
# Makes a Decision

Dating from shortly after he arrived in France, Dr. Benjamin Franklin had evinced solicitude for the unfortunate American prisoners of war in England. As one of the three American Commissioners to the Court of Versailles, his kindly and humane interest had been stirred by their plight to continuous efforts in their behalf. The other Commissioners had given sporadic attention to proposals for exchange, or to have the sufferings of these captives ameliorated, but had been easily discouraged when formal demands upon the British Ministry had been ignored. They had been quite willing then to let the good Doctor take the whole burden upon his aging but still vigorous shoulders. Now that he had become Minister Plenipotentiary, the burden rested there entirely.

And Franklin might well have been discouraged, too, that bleak morning in mid-March, 1779, as, recovering from a severe attack of gout, he sat before the fire in the study of the little house in the rear of M. Le Ray de Chaumont's estate in Passy. Almost nine months had elapsed since his persistency had won reluctant agreement from the Ministry in London to exchange, man for man, American prisoners in England for British prisoners in France.

Tedious negotiations through his old friend, the philanthropic David Hartley, a member of Parliament, had settled the details. The first cartel ship would be sent to Nantes with one hundred Americans taken from Mill Prison, at Plymouth, to be returned with a similar number of Britishers brought into France by American vessels of war. The same cartel would then bring a second load of Americans from Forton Prison, at Portsmouth.

Months had passed, but no cartel ship had appeared. Franklin had about concluded that he and his friend Hartley had been deceived. Delay had been by design—of that he was sure—to give more opportunity for seducing the prisoners, through promises and hardships, to secure their liberty by serving against their country. Hired agents were continual visitors to both prisons, he had learned, telling the captives they had been neglected; that the British government was willing to exchange them, but through his fault it had not been done. These agents had boasted that the American war was about over, with the British victorious, and had threatened each prisoner: Accept the King's pardon and enter on board a man-of-war, or be hanged as a traitor.[1]

Even should the cartel arrive belatedly, Dr. Franklin's problem would be far from solved. He feared there were many more officers and men from Continental vessels, pri-

[1] The effect of this propaganda upon the Americans in Forton Prison, at Portsmouth, England, was evidenced in a letter to Franklin from them in the fall of 1778: "Having been buoyed up with the hopes of an Exchange for Six or seven months we began to Surmise the Reason why it was so long delayed was owing to a non conformity on the part of the British Ministry. Yet they disclaim the charge, Alledging that they have Complyed with every requisite on their part, and that the Completion of it, rests wholly with you: yet as we put no great Confidence in them, we wish to hear the truth from yourself, which will give us infinite Satisfaction." This letter is in the Benjamin Franklin Papers, American Philosophical Society, Philadelphia. Hereafter this collection will be referred to as *Franklin Papers*, APS.

vateers, and letters of marque then imprisoned in England than there were British seamen in his custody for exchange. Such fears were justified. As of mid-March there had been almost five hundred Americans in the two prisons. To off-set these, he had two hundred Britishers in a jail in Brest, and another hundred on board a prison ship in that harbor. The latter were to be dispatched to Nantes for delivery to the British cartel ship, and, as the Doctor remarked dryly, were "not so comfortably accommodated."

Moreover, prize taking in European waters was overwhelmingly in favor of the enemy. Few American war vessels were then cruising abroad and sending prisoners into France, and most of those venturing so far from home had been taken by the enemy.[2] The British navy and privateers were finding rich prey also among lightly armed merchantmen bringing cargoes of wheat, rice, tobacco, and indigo for the Dutch, French, and Spanish markets.[3] Alleviating the sufferings of the few hundred he could exchange meant only that hundreds more would be looking to him for relief he could not supply.

Various and numerous efforts had been made to counteract this disparity in numbers. Until the French treaty in February, 1778, American captains could not retain their prisoners in French ports. The British Ambassador, Lord

[2] From available records it appears that two New Hampshire privateers, the *Hampden* and *General Sullivan,* and a Massachusetts privateer, the *Franklin,* were the only ones operating in European waters in the period, December, 1778 to March, 1779; *Independent Chronicle,* Boston, April 8, 22, 1779; *Public Advertiser,* London, December 14, 1778.

[3] London newspapers recorded prizes of eleven American letters of marque with such cargoes during January and February, 1779. The account of one is typical of all: "Extract of a letter from Falmouth, February 26; 'The Tartar privateer of Folkstone, John Gibra, Commander, has brought into this port the Phoenix, an American brig from Salem, bound to Bourdeaux, with 100 hogsheads of tobacco, besides some indigo, which as times are at present, turns out a valuable prize.'" The London *Chronicle,* March 2–4, 1779.

Stormont, had ignored the Commissioners' first overture for exchange. The second he had "return'd with Insult." [4] So it had been necessary to free all British officers and seamen brought in. By the fall of 1777, some two hundred had been set at liberty, and many more had been dismissed at sea and supplied with vessels to carry them to home ports.

Having been rebuffed by Lord Stormont, the Doctor's next attempt had been through David Hartley, whose interest in reconciliation had made correspondence possible. Some act of generosity and kindness towards American prisoners, such as more humane treatment, or, better still, an exchange, the Doctor had pointed out, would go further towards an accommodation than verbal wishes for peace. "Your King will not reward you for taking this trouble," he had written, "but God will, I shall not mention the good will of America; you have what is better, the applause of your own conscience."

Before Hartley could reply, the Commissioners jointly had addressed Lord North, explaining that, as upwards of five hundred British seamen had been generously treated and set at liberty by American cruisers in European seas, they trusted he would think himself bound "to dismiss an equal number of seamen taken in the service of the United States." The result had been complete silence on the part

4 While Franklin noted upon the letter to the British Ambassador, "return'd with Insult," the Doctor really had the last word. Lord Stormont had returned with the seemingly unopened letter a note reading: "The Kings Ambassador receives no Letters from Rebels but when they come to implore his Majesty's Mercy." Back went the note with a caustic reply, signed by both Franklin and Silas Deane: "In answer to a letter which concerns some of the most material interests of humanity, and of the two nations, Great Britain and the United States of America, now at war, we received the inclosed indecent paper, as coming from your Lordship, which we return for your Lordship's more mature consideration." To make sure the British public read the correspondence, the American Commissioners saw to it that copies were supplied the London newspapers.

of the Prime Minister. A second letter had been drafted, renewing the request "for an immediate exchange of prisoners in Europe," but it had not been sent because Hartley, meanwhile, had reported a proposal from the Board of Admiralty. If Franklin would forward the number and rank of Britishers ready for delivery, an equal number of Americans would be selected from Mill and Forton prisons, each party then sending their prisoners to Calais for exchange.

In accepting this, Franklin again had sought for a broader delivery. He had urged upon Hartley that the British clear their prisons, releasing all Americans. If that should be done, he had given his "solemn Engagement" to deliver to Lord Howe in America, "a Number of your Sailors equal to the Surplus." Negotiations then had droned on; Nantes instead of Calais, one hundred only to be exchanged at a time, no distinction between men taken in Continental service or in merchant vessels, seniority to govern selection, and passports to be issued for cartel ships. But the broader proposal had been rejected. Their Lordships of the Admiralty had determined that it would "be prejudicial to his Majesty's Service to exchange prisoners upon account of Debtor & Creditor."

Refusing to be discouraged by his rebuff, Franklin had another suggestion. If their Lordships would send over two hundred and fifty Americans, he would deliver every Britisher held in France. He had explained it carefully to Hartley: "If the Number we have falls short of the 250, the Cartel ship may take back as many of those she brings as the Deficiency amounts to, delivering no more than she receives. If our Number exceed the 250 we will deliver them all nevertheless, their Lordships promising to send us immediately a Number equal to the Surplus." But their Lordships had the King's consent to the original proposal, and would not presume to ask for an alteration. It would have to be one hundred at a time, man for man, or none.[5]

There it had stood, and the British awareness of their great advantage had again been brought to his attention by his secretary-grandson. Young William Temple Franklin had pointed out a paragraph in a London newspaper of a January date, which had found its way to Passy. A number of benevolent English gentlemen, who in December, 1777, had launched a subscription to relieve the distresses of the American prisoners, had seen their funds dwindling. Before making a new appeal for subscriptions, they had visited the Admiralty to ask John Montagu, Lord Sandwich, whether an exchange would soon take place. The First Lord had received them with great politeness, the paragraph continued, and had informed them, "that though some of the prisoners would probably be exchanged, the greater part would remain for want of a sufficient number of English prisoners in France to exchange in return."

Sandwich's utterances brought to Franklin's mind his own caustic conclusion of a month before, that the Ministry "cannot give up the pleasant idea of having at the end of the war one thousand Americans to hang for high treason." To defeat that unpalatable prospect more prisoners would have to be carried into France. Achieving this would call for more American cruisers, or, at least, cruisers with American commissions, operating in European seas.

One such project was under way. John Paul Jones was

[5] It required four letters from Hartley and three from Franklin over the period, July 10 to October 9, 1778, to conclude the arrangements. Hartley's letters are in Franklin Papers, APS; Franklin's are printed in Francis Wharton (ed.), *The Revolutionary Diplomatic Correspondence of the United States* (Washington, 1889), II, 645, 702, 717. What little has been told of Franklin's disheartening efforts in 1777 and 1778 to secure the exchange of American prisoners in England has been but fragmentary. The Doctor's efforts in behalf of his "unfortunate countrymen," as he uniformly described them, continued to the very end of the war. They deserve to be related, as they show the humanitarian side of his character, which has been much neglected by his biographers.

at L'Orient transforming an old East Indiaman, now called the *Bonhomme Richard,* into a fifty-gun ship of war. But it would be long months before this ship would be ready to sail. The Doctor knew he could commission more vessels to cruise out of French ports. He had the necessary blank commissions. True they were all signed by John Hancock as President of the Continental Congress, and Hancock had retired to Massachusetts more than a year before. That was a detail which might occasion some difficulties.

What chiefly caused him to hesitate, however, was his reluctance to become further involved in naval matters. He felt himself wholly unacquainted with maritime problems, and the distance from Passy to the various ports rendered it most inconvenient to act. Likewise, every Continental ship that had come to a French harbor had required extensive outfitting, and he was no judge either of its necessity or of its cost. Disposing of prizes had produced some tiresome and vexatious arguments in which also he had been involved. Some nine months before, while the American Commissioners still functioned, they had obtained permission from the French Minister of Marine to issue a privateering commission to a sloop fitting at Dunkirk, and containing a mixed crew of Frenchmen, Americans, and Englishmen. It had proved a fiasco. Poreau, Mackenzie & Co., the merchants who had proposed the privateer, had misrepresented its fitness to the Commissioners' agent. Nor had the firm the resources to carry out the equipment desired by the American captain selected to command her. Recriminations had followed. Commission, instructions, and bond, over which much time had been spent, had to be scrapped, and the captain's bill for a useless journey to Dunkirk had to be paid.[6]

6 Franklin's dispatches, from the time he became Minister Plenipotentiary until Congress finally sent a consul to France, are filled with his distaste for maritime affairs, and his reasons are fully set forth. These various

The affair had left an unpleasant taste in Franklin's mouth, and he was loathe to commit himself again. Certainly no more commissions would be issued until the cartel arrived, and the exchange was proceeding as promised. That was why he had declined a more recent request to supply a commission to the burgomaster of Dunkirk, who was equipping a fourteen-gun brig as a privateer. Perhaps a secondary reason was the burgomaster's use of Poreau, Mackenzie & Co. as a reference. Refusal, however, Franklin had ascribed to a desire for fresh orders from Congress.

Now the matter had bobbed up again in a letter just received and lying before him on the escritoire. The writer was Stephen Marchant, a Connecticut-born Boston shipmaster. Marchant had been in Passy in January, after escaping from England via Dunkirk. The Doctor had supplied money for living expenses and a homeward passage, and had expected to hear no more from him. Instead Marchant had returned to Dunkirk, where the burgomaster had offered him command of the brig. All this the captain explained in an atrocious hand and with much misspelling.

"I Receved a Letter that If I Wood Com to Dunkirk I shold have the command off a Priveretere and thinking It a Bad time of the yeare for to goo upon the American kost I Consented for to Com Back," he wrote, "and I Shold Be much a Blig$^d$. to youre honner If you Wood Send the american Commishon Witch It wood Be greatly to me and my Marchants Benafet." He added that he was "Livin at M$^r$. Porrows."

If Marchant's letter might have reopened the subject, the postscript with the return address closed it. Franklin wanted "nothing to do with M$^r$. Porrow," of Poreau, Mac-

dispatches are printed in volumes seven and eight of Albert H. Smyth, *The Writings of Benjamin Franklin* (New York, 1905–1907). The fiasco regarding the sloop at Dunkirk is described in Franklin Papers, APS.

kenzie & Co. So he reached for his quill, dipped it in the inkstand, and scratched out a reply:

> I rec$^d$. yours of the 27$^{th}$ of february requesting a Commission. I had before written to M. Dem-O'hyver [That was a pretty good essay at the burgomaster's name, which was Taverne Demond Dhiver], that it was not in my Power to grant his Request untill I have rec$^d$. fresh Orders from Congress
> But as it is easy for that Gentleman now in time of war to obtain a Commission for you from the Admiralty of France, I wish you would explain to me why you desire rather an American one. I am Sir your humble serv$^t$.[7]

Actually Franklin anticipated no "fresh Orders" from Congress. The American Revolution, in fact, was fought with little or no co-ordination between the efforts in the United States and those in France. It could not be otherwise with ocean crossings requiring at least four weeks eastbound, and, against the prevailing winds, often twice that time westbound; to say nothing of the hazards of storm and enemy interception.[8]

Moreover, in the early months of 1779, the Continental Congress had other problems than instructing its Minister Plenipotentiary in Paris whether he should or should not issue commissions to French-owned, American-captained privateers. James Lovell, of the Committee of Foreign Af-

[7] Stephen Marchant's letter, as well as all subsequent letters from him will be found in Franklin Papers, APS. Franklin's reply, along with all other letters he addressed to the captain are in the American Legation Letter Books in the Library of Congress, hereafter referred to as Letter Books, 1779, or Letter Books, 1780. As they were copied by a young French secretary, M. Lair De Lamotte, the spelling and punctuation are not always as Franklin originally drafted them.

[8] The slowness of communication each way can best be illustrated by two notable examples. Burgoyne's surrender at Saratoga on October 15, 1777, was not heard of by Franklin and his fellow commissioners until December 4, seven weeks later. Similarly, the treaty of alliance with France was signed at Versailles on February 6, 1778, but the news took twelve weeks to reach Congress at York on May 2.

fairs, had felt in December, 1778, that the only important struggle was with the currency. But he was reckoning without Silas Deane, whose address to the "Free and Virtuous Citizens of America" launched a bitter struggle in Congress, which seriously retarded getting on with the war, and practically throttled naval activities. Congress was more interested in getting help from the French fleet in the West Indies for the beleaguered states of South Carolina and Georgia, than advising Franklin of anything. It was content, as Lovell put it in January, in wishing him success and satisfaction in his important agency.

While the Doctor slowly recovered from his attack of gout—even on April 8 there was still "a little remaining indisposition"—he heard that the cartel ship had at last arrived at Nantes. She had brought ninety-seven instead of one hundred Americans from Mill Prison. The reason for the discrepancy was absurd. Carrying out the conceit that the prisoners were still British subjects, George III had issued a pardon early in February to each of the one hundred designated for exchange. By March 15, when they paraded down through Plymouth to the cartel ship, two of their number had died and one was left behind dangerously ill.[9] The three vacancies could not be filled because no others had received royal clemency! But, as Franklin observed, "This Exchange is the more remarkable, as our people were all committed as for high Treason."

Even though unconscionably slow about it, the enemy had shown good faith, so his concern began anew for the Americans who must continue to languish in prison after the supply of Britishers for exchange had been exhausted. When the French Minister of Marine requested that the

[9] The account of the loading and departure of the cartel is detailed in Charles Herbert, *A Relic of the Revolution* (Boston, 1847).

frigate *Alliance*, which had brought Franklin's commission as Minister Plenipotentiary, be held abroad, he was happy to acquiesce, because "she may procure us some more prisoners to exchange the rest of our countrymen." This hope was bolstered by her reputation as an exceedingly fast sailer, and on April 28, he ordered her to join Jones at L'Orient. He had no idea when the squadron gathering there would be ready. A letter from Jones, written at the end of April, had remarked, "Be not discouraged—Our Object will not be lost tho' I Should not be able to put to Sea for two Months to come." [10]

Franklin did not wish to wait for two months. He was in a mood for action. Hence he gave attentive ear to M. Sutton de Clonard, a nobleman of naval bent and with influence at court. M. de Clonard called at Passy early in May, following a trip to Dunkirk, and spoke of a very fine cutter he had seen in that harbor; a cutter being armed with sixteen guns, and which would make an ideal American privateer. Likewise the Count remarked that there were many Irish smugglers idling about Dunkirk. These with some of the escaped Americans, who were continually crossing from Dover, would assure a good crew. Perhaps Dr. Franklin might like to look into it? Having dropped the seed, M. de Clonard let it germinate a few days and then wrote a brief note: "M^r. Stephen Merchant [*sic*] of Boston, is come from Dunkirk to Sollicite your Excellency for an American Commission to Enable him to Command the Cutter of 16 guns which I mention'd to you—I request that you may gratify him therein. This Vessel will have a

[10] Franklin's decision to retain the *Alliance* and join her to John Paul Jones's squadron was suggested by M. de Sartine, French Minister of Marine, and proved the most unfortunate decision the Doctor ever made. The subsequent insubordination of Peter Landais; the charges that the *Alliance* fired into the *Bonhomme Richard* in the famous battle off Scarborough Head, and their aftermaths have supplied naval historians and the innumerable Jones biographers with plenty of controversial material.

very good Crew, American & Irish, as She Sails extremely well, She must do considerable Execution." [11]

Here was the illiterate Marchant back again. Franklin, remembering the Poreau connection and recalling that the captain never had replied to his letter, probably would have refused to consider the request. However, another visitor arrived at Passy with an endorsement of the Count's recommendation. This was Francis Jean Coffyn, Flemish broker and royal interpreter at Dunkirk. For several years Coffyn had been a trustworthy agent for the American Commissioners and had endeared himself to Franklin by the intelligent and sympathetic manner in which he had managed the small fund given him for the relief of escaped prisoners. As the Dunkirk agent had been the one to expose Poreau, Mackenzie & Co. the previous year, the Doctor accepted Coffyn's statement that Marchant was an able but simple-minded seaman, who originally had fallen into bad hands. The owners of the privateer, the agent explained, were the Torris brothers, reputable merchants of Dunkirk. Poreau had nothing to do with her. An ample crew had been recruited, and the owners desired Marchant as her commander. If Dr. Franklin decided to issue the commission, Coffyn would remain in Paris a few days to receive it, and carry it to Dunkirk and administer it personally.

Marchant was given audience and supplied additional data. The cutter was of one hundred and twenty tons burden, and her sixteen carriage guns were all 4-pounders. Outfitting and provisioning were virtually completed for a crew numbering seventy men. As first lieutenant, he was

11 "The Chevalier de Clonard, a second son of a Mr. Sutton, late of the county of Wexford, in Ireland, for services rendered to France during the Seven Year War, was created a Count by Louis XV, by the title of Clonard, a small post town in the County of Meath, just twenty-five miles from Dublin." London *Chronicle*, August 26–29, 1780. Clonard's letter is in the Franklin Papers, APS.

happy to have his former mate in the merchant service, Jonathan Arnold, of Middletown, Connecticut. Franklin listened noncommittally, and sent the captain back to Dunkirk to await a decision.

For twenty-four hours the Doctor considered the matter. Commissioning the privateer, as he knew from past experience, would involve him in many more troubles. On the other hand, encouraging such an armament was the only way he could hope to attain the exchange of more Americans in England. Should this cutter, rejected by him, go forth under a French commission, the prizes she would take would be the property of France; the Britishers she would bring in would be exchanged for Frenchmen. That would be of no service to his countrymen in Mill and Forton prisons. He weighed the inconveniences and annoyances, which might, and most likely would, arise should he issue the commission, against the satisfaction of freeing more men from captivity. As to be expected from Dr. Franklin, his humanitarian interest tipped the scales in behalf of the prisoners.

Once decision was made, action was prompt. He called for a blank commission, a blank bond, and a copy of the oath of allegiance. Young Temple Franklin produced each and listened to his grandfather's directions. The captain's commission was filled in first, then the bond. There were spaces in each for the owners' names to be supplied later. The commission bore John Hancock's signature and was dated October 8, 1777. The Doctor overcame that by endorsing at the bottom: "This Commission is delivered by B. Franklin Minister of the United States at the Court of France to Captain Marchant at Passy, May 19th. 1779."

It was neither delivered at Passy, nor on the date specified; first, because Marchant was not there to receive it, and second, because it was sent by messenger on May 14 to Francis Coffyn, predated to allow for time to reach Dunkirk. "I am directed by my Grand father," Temple Franklin wrote Coffyn, "to transmit you the enclosed Commission for a Privateer, together with the instructions to the Commander and the bond to be signed by the Owners you are directed carefully to attend to the filling up of the Blanks both in the Commission and Bond." Temple added that the oath of allegiance should be taken by the captain in the agent's presence before the commission was delivered.

The instructions Franklin wrote himself. They were explicit and to the point. Marchant was to bring in all the prisoners possible, "because they serve to relieve so many of our Country-men from their Captivity in England." With that singleness of purpose as a benediction, the Doctor launched the *Black Prince* upon her career.[12]

12 A copy of Stephen Marchant's commission, taken from one of his prizemasters, found its way eventually into the British Admiralty Papers in the Public Records Office, London. William Temple Franklin's letter, sending the commission to Francis Coffyn, is in Letter Books, 1779, and Coffyn's acknowledgment is in Franklin Papers, APS.

## CHAPTER II

# *Conspiracy at Dunkirk*

THE STEPS TAKEN to obtain an American commission for the *Black Prince* had involved an amusing and harmless little conspiracy at Dunkirk. The participants were John Torris, his brother Charles, a silent partner in the Torris firm, and Luke Ryan, whose smuggling cutter *Friendship* had now become the privateer. Ryan had selected the new name because of her sleek lines, black sides, and almost legendary reputation as one of the swiftest vessels that ever had run a smuggling cargo. Perhaps, too, he saw some analogy to that Black Prince of English chivalry, whose deeds echoing down the centuries were traditions that still stirred the youth of Flanders.

He and the Flemish merchants, the brothers Torris, were no strangers. From their warehouse in past years, Ryan had shipped many a cask of wine and many a canister of tea, which, without benefit of excise, had found its way into the British Isles. For that reason he had come to John Torris when the cutter reached Dunkirk. He had described the deed which had made him and his crew outlaws, and had told of their determination to turn to privateering. He had proposed that the merchant purchase a half interest in the cutter. For that interest, Torris was to provide

money to convert her to warlike purposes, provision her
for a three months' cruise, and advance wages enough to
satisfy the men brought from Ireland.

Torris had accepted Ryan's offer with alacrity. Louis
XVI in the preceding July had authorized and encouraged
letters of marque and reprisal. The merchant flattered himself that M. de Sartine, Minister of Marine, and M. de
Chardon, Procurer-General for the Council of Prizes, were
well inclined in his favor. He would have no trouble in
securing a French commission for the cutter. To that Ryan
had interposed an emphatic "No!" While he knew French,
his crew spoke naught but English, and that with an Irish
brogue. With a French commission, if taken, they would
have a devil of a job passing as Frenchmen. He wanted
an American commission. Then, if captured, they would
claim to be citizens of the United States and let the British
try to prove them otherwise!

How to obtain an American commission was a puzzler.
Torris could not conceive of an American minister bestow-
ing a captain's commission upon an Irish smuggler, no
matter how highly he might be recommended. He based
this opinion upon an experience his friend Francis Coffyn
had related to him not so long ago. The agent had proposed such a commission be granted to a Christopher Far-
ran of Rush, a noted smuggler, who had a cutter carrying
twelve guns, and who was "an attach'd friend to the american cause." Coffyn's lengthy letter of endorsement to the
American Commissioners had not even been acknowledged.

Nonetheless, Torris and Ryan were in agreement that
the agent should be approached and asked how to secure
a commission from Dr. Franklin for a privateer which
would be manned only by Americans and Irishmen. Not
knowing what Coffyn's attitude would be, they decided to
divulge as little as possible to him. The past history of the

*Black Prince* should not be disclosed, nor Ryan's desire to command her.

Torris's interview with Coffyn gave them something to consider. The agent still remembered his unpleasant experience with Poreau, Mackenzie & Co. the previous year. He related that story, and added that Dr. Franklin had recently refused a request for a privateering commission made by the burgomaster of Dunkirk. The worthy American who was to have commanded that privateer had just been to see him. He felt very sorry for this Captain Marchant, a fine seafarer who had been misled and, when the commission had been denied, ill-treated by the burgomaster and his partner, Mr. Poreau. Perhaps Mr. Torris would like to consider this captain for the privateer he had in mind? If so, Mr. Coffyn, because of his great confidence in Mr. Torris, would be glad to recommend it to Dr. Franklin.

Thus it happened that the Flemish merchant and Ryan met Marchant and quickly sized him up. They rated him as a man of impressive appearance and with a large ego, but a somewhat empty head. Adroitly handled he would make a good cat's-paw. If Franklin refused to grant a commission to an Irish smuggler—and they feared he would—Stephen Marchant could be the "ostensible" captain of the *Black Prince.* As one of the owners, Ryan could serve on board as second captain. Whereupon, they engaged the American and even permitted him to sign up his former mate as first lieutenant. Francis Coffyn was vastly pleased to have his recommendation accepted. So was M. de Clonard, who had arrived in Dunkirk and was visibly impressed with the privateer, her commander and crew. Luke Ryan kept discreetly out of sight until Clonard, Marchant, and Coffyn, one after the other, departed for Passy to press their suit for the coveted commission.

The captain, of course, was the first to return. He could

report a kindly reception by Dr. Franklin, but was no wiser than before he had set out. They would have to await arrival of Francis Coffyn. Instead of the agent, one of his clerks ended the suspense on May 19. The commission had been granted. Coffyn, due to "a Sudden indisposition and then some unexpected business," had been detained in Paris. Rather than delay the armament, he was happy to send along commission, instructions, bond and oath of allegiance to be properly filled in and the bond, and oath returned to him.

Absence of the agent made it far simpler for the conspirators. Coffyn might have asked questions when a mythical Peter Bernardson was listed in commission and bond as a part owner of the *Black Prince*. The clerk, however, had no suspicions although Bernardson existed only in Luke Ryan's imagination. The other owner was given as Charles Torris, the firm's silent partner. John Torris' and Ryan's names appeared in neither document. Marchant, right hand resting upon Torris' French Bible, took the oath of allegiance to the United States and each of its thirteen member states, vowing that he owed no obedience to King George and swearing that he would "to the Utmost of my Power Support, maintain, and defend the Said united States against the said King and his Heirs and Successors, and his and their Abettors, Assistants and Adherents . . . So help me God!" The oath, thus solemnly administered and properly witnessed, and the bond, duly executed and signed, were turned over to Coffyn's clerk to be forwarded to Paris.

To this point John Torris' name had not appeared in the transactions. Coffyn had identified the owners simply as the Torris brothers. When Dr. Franklin received and examined the bond he would find only Charles Torris' signature. Therefore, John Torris felt it encumbent to introduce himself to Passy and inform the Doctor that the

affairs of the privateer were in competent hands. Likewise
Torris was disturbed by a decision he attributed to Marchant, but instigated by Ryan, to cruise after the British
packets plying between Dover and Calais. In his quaint
English, the merchant wondered "whether these wou'd not
Prove wrong Steps against the Intentions or determina-
tions of yourself & Congress." He had prefaced his inquiry
by explaining that he was sole agent for Marchant and the
entire crew of the *Black Prince,* as well as for the owners,
and was himself "Deeply Interested" in her. As his agency
included sale of all prizes and any other transactions involved in her operations, he had charged himself with
acquainting Dr. Franklin of all that went on.

Torris had examined commission and instructions and
could find no exceptions to the taking of all British vessels.
If the packets were not to be legitimate prizes, he felt sure
it would have been mentioned somewhere; nevertheless,
he was still dubious. "I beseech you will be so kind to give
me, or M^r. Marchant, your own Private Directions how to
act," he continued. "My Character in Business & Titles
[The titles were not specified] answer for my Discretion
& gratefull use of your generous Informations,  But if you
do not think Proper to favour me with an Answer I beseech you will do it forthwith to M^r. Marchant Directed to
my Care." A reply by return of the post, said he, would
arrive in Dunkirk before the *Black Prince* would sail.[1]

To make way for an American captain and first lieutenant, the Irish officers of the *Black Prince* had to step
down in rank. Ryan had told them why, with assurances
that Marchant and Arnold were figureheads. Necessary adjustments were made, the demoted men being much

[1] All the numerous letters of John Torris and Francis Coffyn are in
Franklin Papers, APS. In reading them, it is easy to trace the conspiracy,
which led Torris and Luke Ryan to accept Marchant as the nominal commander of the *Black Prince.*

amused and quite willing to give lip service to the "ostensible" commander. The rearrangement was never clearly stated. Perhaps the best idea was given by a British prisoner, who later remembered some of those on board. He recalled Marchant and two lieutenants, Arnold and Bennet, who, he was told, were Americans. Bennet was Edward Macatter, who was prone to call himself an American although he was born in county Cork and probably had never been west of Cape Clear.

The Britisher named others: "Ellick Weldin—Connir —Doolan officers all Irish—W^m. Knight, Sailing Master and Pilot—his Country not known—Ryan, Owner, Irish —Dixon, Boatswain Irish—Kelly Master at Arms Irish— McCloud Gunners Mate Country not known—Christopher Kelly, Michael Morgan, Bartholomew Mulvany all Irish Sailors—Christopher Hoar and—Smith Country not known —Cornelly Steward Irish." Some of these can be better identified. "Ellick Weldin" was Alexander Weldin, who had been second mate of the smuggler. "Doolin" was Patrick Dowlin, and "Connir" was Thomas Connor, both master's mates. The "Kelly Master at Arms" had been baptized Timothy and also acted as clerk.

Manning the *Black Prince* had presented no problem. About thirty-six Rushmen had come to Dunkirk in her, and there were many smugglers in the port and out of employ. Some were Irish and some English, and all were willing to sign up. The common practice had been employed; an advance before sailing, as a kind of bounty to each man, proportionate to his rank on board. Torris had paid out a total of around 20,000 livres. In return the crew had agreed that the advances would be charged against prize shares, but that the cost of the outfit of the privateer should be deducted before prize shares were computed. Should there be no prizes, or an insufficient number, the advances need not be refunded. Each officer and man signed an oath of allegiance similar to that administered to Marchant.

Extensive alterations had been made to enable the former smuggler to carry and fight so large a crew. She was a good sixty-five feet in length, and her beam was about twenty feet. The hold, which had boasted so many valuable cargoes, was now planked over from the forward galley to the after platform, providing a berth deck with little headroom, but sufficient in length and breadth to sling fifty or more hammocks. On the after platform the number of cubbyholes for officers had been increased by the simple expedient of decreasing the size of each. Even the captain's cabin had been invaded with the addition of a berth for Luke Ryan, who rated it as an owner, if not as second captain.

In her former trade the *Black Prince* had carried fewer weapons than the armament she now bore. To show her enlarged battery of sixteen 4-pounders and thirty swivels, additional gunports had been cut and more swivel stocks erected against the bulwarks. She was still painted black, had no figurehead, and was sloop-rigged. In those days the difference between sloop and cutter rigging seems to have been a short fixed bowsprit as against a long, movable one, and a single headsail.[2]

By the beginning of June she was ready and Marchant and Ryan were impatient to get to sea. There had been no word by return of post from Franklin. Torris persuaded the reluctant captain to defer departure, expecting early instructions from Passy. Days passed and no letter arrived. At the end of a week, prodded by Ryan, Marchant announced that he interpreted no reply as a clear approba-

---

2 The description of the *Black Prince* and her crew is supplied by two affidavits and numerous letters about her in the Public Records Office, Admiralty Papers; also by the account of a person who had left Dunkirk right after she had sailed on her first cruise, London *Chronicle*, July 3–6, 1779.

tion of his intention to take the Dover-Calais packets, and that he would sail on the first fair wind.

Torris could do no more, but his doubts still lingered. He again wrote to Franklin, explaining that the captain "is fully persuaded your Excellency's Justice wou'd not Leave him in any Dilemma & that your Silence Shows you'll grant him all assistance to make these Prises be Condemned to his Proffit." If Marchant succeeded, his Excellency immediately would be informed, and, in the meantime, the merchant awaited any commands.

The *Black Prince* sailed on Saturday, June 12, steering to the westward from Dunkirk Road.

Morning, noon, and sometimes in the evenings during the first ten days in June, Dr. Franklin was employing himself and his grandson in the arduous business of writing many letters to America. An opportunity for a safe conveyance—the French frigate that was to take a new ambassador to the United States—was not to be neglected. Consequently other matters were neglected, among them the two letters from John Torris. Both were filed unanswered, and the Doctor's later lame explanation arouses suspicion that they were also unread.

Certainly the affairs of the *Black Prince* were furtherest from his thoughts until they were recalled forcibly on June 17. Francis Coffyn forwarded the bond and Marchant's oath of allegiance, and apologized for not having delivered them in person. The illness which had prevented the agent from returning to Dunkirk had confined him to his chamber in Paris since the first of the month. He concluded with word that the privateer was already out cruising.

Later that day, a note from the Chevalier de Baudouin, secretary to the Minister of Marine, sent Franklin ransacking his files. The note disclosed the French intelligence service at its best. M. de Sartine had been advised, Baudouin wrote, that an American corsair was planning to interrupt the Dover and Calais packets; that the captain had written to the American Minister to inform him of this design, and having received no reply, interpreted the silence as consent.

"M^r. Sartine instantly begs your Excellency to write promptly and as strongly as possible to this captain," the Chevalier continued, "that he is to abstain from attacking any Dover to Calais packet; this communication can in truth be of some usefulness to our common enemies, but truly in these respects, as your Excellency will guess with no trouble, it is advantageous to us, and even necessary, and I do not doubt that the French Court will keep it as long a time as the London court wishes to let it continue."

From Franklin's acknowledgment, it seems he had not yet located the correspondence, but, with his amazing mental agility, had found a plausible reason to cover his negligence. He had not attended closely to the captain's letter he admitted. The reason was his supposition that, if the packets were under government protection they would if stopped produce that protection which would suffice. However, he would write at once and forbid the captain meddling with them.

Later that day he discovered that Marchant had not written to him at all; that it was John Torris who had addressed him, not once, but twice on the subject. So to Torris he sent, a bit belatedly, the orders that gentleman had so earnestly desired, and which bore out the merchant's premonitions. Franklin's explanation for not previously replying was similar to the one he had given to M. Baudouin. But, "as an Interruption of the Correspondence between the two Nations, would be disagreeable to the government as being prejudicial to Commerce," he wanted Captain Marchant advised that he would not be countenanced in any such an enterprise. Moreover, if the captain should persist and take a packet or two, "they will not be condemned to him." [3]

This was getting off to a bad start. Already Franklin was experiencing some of the difficulties he had visualized in his privateering venture. He could congratulate himself, though, that several weeks before he had again urged upon the Marine Committee of Congress the necessity of appointing consuls for the several European seaports. Such men could, as he had pointed out, far better transact maritime business, "relieve your Minister at this Court from a great Deal of Trouble, and leave him at Liberty to attend Affairs of more general Importance." If and when such consuls were appointed he certainly would refer to them the problems of the *Black Prince*. The Doctor would realize in due time, however, that his reliance upon such relief was badly misplaced. [4]

[3] The misunderstanding about taking the English packets is covered fully in John Torris' letters of June 8 and 16, 1779; the Chevalier de Baudoin's note to Franklin of June 17, 1779, both in Franklin Papers, APS, and Franklin's letter of June 18, 1779, in Letter Books, 1779.

[4] Congress eventually responded to Franklin's appeals and appointed William Palfrey, who had been Paymaster General of the Continental Army as United States Consul to France. Palfrey sailed from Philadelphia in the ship *Shillala,* Captain Alexander Holmes, in December, 1780, but the vessel was lost in her passage with all on board. In October, 1781, a successor was named, Thomas Barclay, who reached France in November of that year. By that time, however, Franklin had weathered his woes without benefit of consul.

CHAPTER III

# The First Cruise—
# in the English Channel

THE INITIAL CRUISE of the *Black Prince* began
on a bright and warm June morning. A moderate downchannel breeze caught her as she came out of Dunkirk
Road, helping her along famously towards the English
shore. American, British, and French colors were in her
flag locker but she showed none of them. Her guns housed,
ports closed, she sought to pass for a simple coaster, but
was so "full of men," as the saying went, that the thin dis-
guise would not bear up under close scrutiny. A crew of
seventy simply could not be concealed in so small a vessel.
Officers and men were cramped for space whether on deck
or below.

Luke Ryan had agreed with John Torris to give Stephen
Marchant his head. They would defer to him as long as
he conducted the cruise in conformity to instructions and
demonstrated his ability to cope with situations as they
arose. Luke would exert all of his charm to ingratiate himself with the American and learn how best to influence
him without seeming to do so. It was no part of the scheme
to show their hand until time and events made it desirable.

By great good or ill fortune—depending upon whether

it was from Dr. Franklin's or their point of view—the
*Black Prince* missed the Calais-Dover packets. Her first
encounter the morning she sallied forth from Dunkirk was
with a brig of Portuguese register. The boarding officer
reported a cargo of "English Manufactured Goods." As
this might prove contraband, Marchant put a prize crew
on board to carry her into Calais where the Admiralty
Court could decide. Late that night a Danish brig was
brought to and searched. She was bound for Dublin with
lumber. Here surely was a prize. They were off Calais, so
he escorted her into that port in the morning. The Judge
of the Admiralty ruled promptly that neither Portuguese
nor Danish brig was a legitimate prize and dismissed them.
Much chagrined and Dunkirk being but twenty-five miles
distant, Marchant sent a note overland to Torris telling
of his lack of success.

On Sunday evening, June 13, he weighed and stood out,
heading across towards Dover. Toward midnight they fell
in with a large ship beating upchannel. They took her to
be an English merchantman en route to London and gave
chase. She was easy to overhaul, came to promptly on their
hail, and proved another disappointment, a Dutch West
Indiaman bound to Amsterdam. She mounted enough
heavy guns to have blown the *Black Prince* out of the water
had she been an enemy. Monday they sailed southwestward
close in with the English coast, boarding several prospec-
tive prizes only to find them neutral Dutch and Swedish
ships. One vessel, appearing to be British, sheered off at
sight of them and ran for shore. They were close enough
to identify her as a ten-gun cutter, but could not come
within gunshot.

Farther down the Channel, after rounding Denge Ness
in the false dawn of Tuesday, six vessels were discovered
ahead. Main-, fore-, topsails, and jib were set in pursuit—
every stitch of canvas the *Black Prince* could carry. They

overtook and spoke one of the six—a small dogger not worth bothering with—and continued after the rest, all brigs and four of them armed. Their quarry by then was close under Beachy Head. By eight o'clock, when the privateer came within range, the water had shoaled to six fathoms. "We engaged them for 2 hours & Chattered them so much they were forced to run on shore," was Marchant's jubilant report. He followed them into a small bay when a British fort opened fire and the lead line showed but three fathoms of water.

The day's excitement had just begun. Running out of the bay, they spotted another small fleet coming down around Beachy Head, coasters under strong convoy. Five of His Majesty's cutters could be seen in close attendance, and one of these detached herself to investigate. Marchant stood not upon the order of his going, but clapped on all sail and fled westward, the enemy cutter hard on his heels. The *Black Prince* outsailed her pursuer until she unfortunately lost her topmast irons, forcing down her topsail. That changed the picture. The British vessel gained rapidly. Marchant plied his stern chases for half an hour to no avail. The enemy came abreast, so close that her captain, before pouring in a broadside, called out something which was heard but not understood. No damage was done by either words or shot. *The Black Prince*'s 4-pounders answered with a far more effective fire. Her Irish seamen, in the space of an hour, gave the cutter four guns to one, and heard the Britishers "Crey most dreadfully." After five or six broadsides, their opponent sheered off. "We have great reason to think that there is a great many of them both kill'd & wounded," Marchant exulted. He made repairs and pursued, chasing the cutter until she regained her fleet. A frigate off the starboard bow gave them pause. They concluded the busy day by heading out to sea to avoid her, and standing westward down the Channel.

Exchanging blows with British war vessels, while much
to be commended, was not accomplishing the purposes of
the cruise—prizes for themselves and prisoners for Dr.
Franklin. Out of his smuggling experiences, Luke Ryan
knew the sea lanes around England and Ireland and could
point to brighter prospects once west of the Lizard. The
waters they were approaching, between the Isle of Wight
and Cape la Hague, were apt to be overpopulous, he remarked, with enemy cruisers maintaining communications
with England's Channel Islands. A frigate off the weather
bow on Wednesday afternoon gave point to his observa-
tion. They spied her just after speaking with a Spanish
merchantman who informed them that the fleet of Spain
had sailed from Ferrol; a bit of intelligence of no practical
use. Either they were unobserved from, or disdained by
the frigate; so the *Black Prince* resumed her course un-
disturbed.

Daybreak Thursday morning found them some four
leagues south of Peveral Point on the Dorsetshire coast,
and disclosed a vast armada about ten miles away in the
northeast. Marchant and Ryan knew it to be the much
heralded British Grand Fleet, and thanked their good fortune that the *Black Prince* was too far off to be noticed.
The fleet, which had sailed from Spithead the day before,
was proceeding majestically downchannel. Marchant
veered away to the southeastward to put even more distance between them. By noon even the huge ships of the
line were hull down. Not until nightfall, however, did the
captain venture to resume his way westward. All through
Friday, June 18, in fine weather, they continued their
course, seeing nothing more of the Grand Fleet, nor, for
that matter, of any merchantmen. That night they
rounded Lizard Point, some half-dozen leagues off shore,
and entered the area where Ryan had predicted better
luck.

Saturday morning began unpropitiously with another frigate on their weather quarter. Marchant steered southeast by east until clear of her; then tacked about into the northwest. Most of the day distant ships were in sight. They were frigates and one or two ships of the line—probably the rear division of the Grand Fleet—all sailing westerly and heeding the *Black Prince* not at all. Towards sunset, with Land's End six leagues away to the northwest, they again saw the whole fleet. It was far off to the south of them—between them and the French coast—and seemed to be bearing westward. They dismissed it, and kept on toward the jutting peninsula marking the western end of old England.

Close to Land's End about twilight, they took their first prize, the brig *Blessing,* from Tenby in Wales, in ballast. An hour later they boarded another brig, the *Liberty.* She, too, was in ballast, from Teignmouth in Devon. Just before midnight they bagged the sloop *Sally* with a cargo of coal from Swansea in Wales, for Falmouth. Unsuspecting British merchantmen continued to fall prey to them. The brig *Hampton,* loaded with coal and earthenware and bound from Liverpool for London, was taken at two o'clock Sunday morning, and the sloop *Elizabeth* an hour later. The latter, with a cargo of coal, oats and butter, had been bound from Carmarthan in Wales for Falmouth. After day dawned, still coasting around Land's End, they took the small brig *Three Sisters.* She was in ballast from Bideford in Devon. In two more hours they had a seventh prize, the brig *Orange Tree,* carrying a cargo of peas (King's provisions) from London for Cork.

By now the prisoners had become an embarrassment. About thirty-five Englishmen had been removed from the prizes and the hold would not contain them all. Some, perforce, mingled with the crew, a precarious situation were a British war vessel encountered. Even allowing for twenty-one men in prize crews sent to six of the vessels, the *Black Prince* was overcrowded. Ryan suggested a solution: Ransom the *Three Sisters,* which was in tow unmanned and of little value, and put most of the captives in her. He offered to prepare a ransom bill and Marchant agreed. A price of seventy-three pounds was set upon the brig, "she being but a poor vessel." The bill specified that the ransom money should be paid "to the Order of M$^r$. John Torris Merchant in Dunkirk, or to his Order in London." For security they held the *Three Sisters'* mate. Fourteen of the prisoners were retained. The rest of them boarded the *Three Sisters,* which sailed with Marchant's endorsement on the brig's copy of the ransom bill: "Gentlemen, French or Americans—Be pleased to let the Bearer Capt$^n$ George Crooker pass for the Space of six Days from the Date of these Presents."

Just after the *Three Sisters* separated from them, they sighted a brig to seaward and stood for her. Later it would be claimed they decoyed her to them and then fired upon her under British colors, a charge they would heatedly deny. Be that as it may, they boarded her, the brig *Goodwill,* from London for Waterford in Ireland with a cargo of porter, iron, and dry goods. She was the eighth prize taken within twenty-four hours and richest of them all. Marchant had sent the other vessels off for France. Because of her value, he decided to convoy in the *Goodwill.* Her crew of seven was removed and four of his Irishmen put in her. He took her in tow, and sailed for the French coast.

Morlaix on the northern shore of the Brittany peninsula was the destination as it was of the six prizes that had preceded them. All Sunday afternoon and evening they ran southeasterly across the English Channel. During that night they passed undetected through the fringe of the Grand Fleet lying south of the Isles of Scilly. Monday afternoon they sighted the Isle of Bas to the northward of their haven. Then the inevitable frigate appeared to leeward. In her company was a vessel quickly identified as the sloop *Elizabeth.* That boded ill for the rest of the prizes. Their course brought them closer to the frigate, which hoisted French colors. No one was deceived. They hauled their wind, the *Goodwill* still in tow, and stood due eastward, paralleling the island some three leagues off shore. "Y*e* fregate Soon put about after us," Marchant reported, "So we kept him in play untill night and then Cast the Brigg off and Boore doune upon her and he Gave us Chase, and by that means the Brigg Got Clear." Their pursuer, Captain George Farmer, in His Majesty's frigate *Quebec,* admitted later that the advantage the privateer had in short tacks enabled her to evade him in the darkness. At that, the chase lasted six hours.

With the American flag flying for the first time since the cruise began, the *Black Prince* sailed into Morlaix Road on Tuesday afternoon, June 22, ten days after her departure from Dunkirk. She saluted the fort and kept on up the river to the town. The *Goodwill* had beaten her in by an hour. None of the other prizes had appeared, although one was reported in a port seven leagues to the eastward. Marchant hoped it was true, "for if they Should be retaken we Shou'd be very Short of men, for there is 21 of the Best of the Crew on board of them." [1]

But, alas, it was not true. Not only the *Elizabeth,* but the other five prizes as well had been retaken, and by the *Quebec,* the same frigate that had hounded them into Morlaix. The twenty-one Irishmen headed by Bryan Rooney and Edward Duff, gunner's and boatswain's mates respectively, had wound up in a prison on Guernsey into which island the recaptured vessels had been carried.

[1] Marchant supplied two accounts of his first cruise in the *Black Prince.* One went to Franklin and the other to Torris. Torris forwarded his letter from Marchant to the Doctor, so the latter had the story almost in duplicate. Both accounts are in Franklin Papers, APS.

This disheartening information reached Morlaix within twenty-four hours, but after Marchant had written to John Torris. It would be more precise to say that he had dictated the letter to Timothy Kelly, one of Ryan's better-educated Irishmen, who prided himself upon a fair hand and who misspelled far fewer words than did the captain.[2] Marchant's letter had advised Torris of the results of the cruise, asked that someone be sent from Dunkirk to handle prize matters, and estimated that "If all the prises was to arrive Safe They would be worth more than £ 10000 Sterling." This was counting prematurely, although the *Goodwill* alone was figured as worth about half of that total.

By the time Marchant neared the end of a second letter —to Dr. Franklin—he had the bad news. To his grief, "Six of our prizes were retaken by the English together with 21 of my Men," he informed the Doctor. With so many prisoners, and his crew weakened by manning prizes, he had been "Constrained to sett Some of them at Liberty and put them in the Ransomed Brig." He had kept twenty-one prisoners, which he had brought in with him, and this, he concluded, "is a brief Account of my Cruize from the 12th untill the 23d Inst June."

After that Marchant had to dictate another letter to tell John Torris that all six missing prizes were lost to them. He counted it fortunate that the number of prisoners brought into Morlaix corresponded exactly with the number of his men in British custody. Through Torris' influence with Franklin, he believed they could be exchanged immediately, man for man. Rather it was Ryan's belief, Marchant's dictation, and Kelly's pen which solicited the

[2] Timothy Kelly identified himself in the summer of 1780 to Franklin, thus: "Repeatedly I have wrote to your Exellency when in the Black Prince Privateer of Boston under the commands in both Cruizes of Capt Marchant and Dowlin wherein we took Prizes & Ransoms to a Considerable Amount. the Names of sd. Prizes as Clerk of our former Privateer I always sent your Excellency an Account thereof." Kelly's letter is in Franklin Papers, APS.

merchant "to use y$^r$. Endeavours as Soon as possible to have the Cartel Made." Until he could get them back or replace them, his cruise would be much retarded. The ensuing boastful promise was unquestionably Marchant's own: "you may Depend upon it I shall upon all Occasions that Offers to Serve my Owners myself and Crew Act with Courage prudence and Conduct." Serving his country seems to have been of such little importance as to need no mention. Meantime, the prisoners were lodged in Morlaix jail to await whatever disposition Franklin or Torris might order.

Benjamin Franklin was relieved to find Marchant's report upon the cruise of the *Black Prince* written in a legible hand. The letter had reached Passy towards the end of June. He had opened it with misgivings, wondering if it would be decipherable and what ill-tidings it might bring. Doubts still lingered about the captain despite the assurances of Clonard and Francis Coffyn. Also the Doctor had disquieting fears that his belated orders regarding the Dover-Calais packets might have arrived too late. He was agreeably surprised to see that an amanuensis had been employed, and both pleased and disappointed by the contents: pleased to learn the privateer had taken eight British merchantmen, with no packets included, and had brought in twenty-one prisoners; disappointed to read that six prizes with twenty-one men had been recaptured, and that Marchant had liberated so many Englishmen in the ransomed brig. It was ironical that the first effort to accumulate more prisoners for exchange had been nullified by the loss of an equal number of men. At that rate, the total of unfortunates in Mill and Forton prisons would never diminish.

Shortly he had a superabundance of information about the cruise, as John Torris forwarded, with one of his own, the first letter Marchant had written to Dunkirk. Torris' report was that he had sent John Diot, a trusted clerk, express to Morlaix to handle prize matters and "advise your Excellency of all that Passes." The merchant requested Franklin to instruct the captain in the disposition of the prisoners, and in the management of the ransom payment for the *Three Sisters*. As this letter was written before hearing of the loss of the prizes, Torris was almost clairvoyant in suggesting that Marchant be encouraged to ransom more vessels rather than risk good men in bringing them in.

A second communication from the Dunkirk merchant reached Passy on July 3. It enclosed the captain's letter asking for immediate exchange of the twenty-one captured crew members of the *Black Prince*. "I warmly Join my request for the Exchange herein mentioned," Torris wrote, "hoping your Excellency, guided by your Justice, will employ her generous offices to Procure this Exchange as soon as Possible." He was expressing proper sentiments with an improper gender.

Torris had more to suggest. He wanted M. de Sartine prevailed upon to order all possible recruiting assistance given at Morlaix "to the good, honest & brave People of the Privateer." If that could not be accomplished, then, perhaps the Minister of Marine would "order some Kings ships to Cruise on the Coast, to Protect her & her Success & defend the French Shore for the attempt & harm done by our Bold Ennemy." Franklin was amused. Calling upon the French navy to protect an American privateer while she forayed against British shipping was, to say the least, a unique request.

The Doctor reflected a long time as to what he should tell Stephen Marchant. Under no circumstances could he effect an immediate exchange of the *Black Prince*'s men, nor, in justice to those who had languished many months in British prisons, would he try to. But he did not wish to dampen the captain's enthusiasm, and he wanted the privateer out again with a minimum of delay. There was a possibility that the second cartel, due any day at Nantes, might provide some hands. But Nantes was a considerable distance from Morlaix. He could suggest it, at least. Then there was the liberation of prisoners. He appreciated that the cutter was small; that she could scarcely accommodate her own crew let alone prisoners. Yet every man set free meant one less available to redeem an American from England. All these matters had been resolved before, on July 4, he penned his letter to Marchant.

Franklin began in a complimentary manner: "I see you have been both diligent and successful. The Misfortune of having several of your Prises retaken was what you could not help." He could not procure the particular exchange desired (and he underlined particular) but, "in the general Exchange which is going on your Men will be discharged in their Turn." The prisoners brought in should be delivered to the commissary at Morlaix. A cartel ship was due from England (he did not say where) with one hundred Americans, and "you will be at liberty to take as many of them as you may want to make up your Loss and as shall be willing to go with you." He gave no directions about collecting ransom money. That was the concern of owners and crew. The United States had no monetary interest in it. He cared not whether they ransomed prizes or brought them into port. But a ransomed vessel by no means meant that her entire crew, save a lone ransomer, should be released. Franklin cited the *Three Sisters* to make his point.

"You should if possible have brought in all your Prisoners except what were necessary to sail the ransomed Vessel," he chided the captain, "because they serve to relieve so many of our Countrymen from their Captivity in

England." Necessity, no doubt, could be offered in apology, but he hoped that Marchant would hereafter follow instructions to bring in prisoners. "If you should again be obliged to dismiss some," he concluded, "take their Engagements in writing to procure the Discharge of an equal Number from the Prisoners in England."

In suggesting paroles at sea, Franklin had no knowledge that the British would be willing to exchange on that basis, but in view of the limited capacity of the *Black Prince*, it was worth trying.[3]

3 Until Franklin authorized Marchant to take paroles at sea, the practice among American captains, cruising in European waters, had been to release unconditionally all prisoners they could not, or did not care to carry in. For example, according to the *Public Advertiser* of April 23, 1779, the *Black Prince* of Salem—not to be confused with the Doctor's *Black Prince*—had taken four vessels, and one of them was given to the crews and arrived at Castle Townsend in Ireland. Subsequently in May, the *Pilgrim* privateer released 120 prisoners in the last of five prizes she had taken, and these men arrived at Waterford. This account also appeared in the *Public Advertiser* on May 24, 1779.

## CHAPTER IV

# The Second Cruise— in the Bristol Channel

STILL UNDERMANNED, but graved and fully provisioned, the *Black Prince* dropped down into Morlaix Road before the middle of July. Torris' clerk, John Diot, had come from Dunkirk to handle the prize *Goodwill*, but was of no help in securing additional hands. Franklin's letter had suggested filling up the crew from an expected cartel ship, but no one had heard of her arrival in any French port. Little effort was wasted looking for her, which was fortunate, for the cartel at that time had not yet departed from Plymouth Sound.

Three Frenchmen had been signed on—a surgeon and a carpenter and his mate. The muster roll then showed fifty-two officers and men. Marchant resorted to enlisting some of his British prisoners. It was a dangerous practice, and contravened Franklin's aim in commissioning the privateer. The captain, for want of men, was obliged to take twelve prisoners "at their own Request they being good Seamen." That was what he told the Doctor in expressing his "Infinite Satisfaction to find y$^r$. Excellency Approves of my Conduct in my last Cruize." One of the Britishers had a different story. Marchant had come to them in prison, and, when they complained of ill usage by their French jailers, had promised that "if they would go along with him he would put them on Shore somewhere in their own Country."

Whatever the inducement may have been, the *Black Prince* now had sixty-four on board, including, as John Diot reported, "M$^r$ Luke Ryan one of the owners." She sailed from the roadstead on Thursday, July 15, in clear, pleasant weather, and stood northwestward for the English shore. The Grand Fleet had gone back up the Channel to Tor Bay. No cruising frigates appeared as the privateer steered directly for Land's End. Winds continued favorable and the fifty leagues were traversed in twenty-four hours.

The first encounter—with a neutral Dutchman—cost them a man who was drowned in boarding. After that misfortune they rounded Land's End and, off Cape Cornwall in rapid succession, took two brigs and a sloop. They were so close to the Cornish shore that the exploit was witnessed from the cape. One of the prizes was a collier from the Welsh coal mines, the brig *Lucy*, Swansea for St. Ives. She was almost in sight of her destination when captured. Another was the sloop *John*, carrying a cargo of copper and oil from Basset's Cove, otherwise known as Portreath, a few miles beyond St. Ives Bay, for Bristol. The third was the brig *Ann*, with beef and other provisions, bound from Bideford in Devon around to Plymouth. Marchant entered in his journal, for Franklin's future edification, that he had sunk all three, "they not worth bringing in (I not having Men that cou'd be depended upon)." Actually, he did nothing of the sort. He ransomed them for amounts ranging from seventy to three hundred guineas.

Rather than burden himself with prisoners so early in the cruise, he availed himself of the privilege given by the Doctor to extract sea paroles. These were prepared by

Ryan, who, in seeking to avoid loopholes, produced an involved and tortuous sentence. It set forth that those signing "have been Prisoners on board the Black Prince privateer of Boston, Cap^t. Stephen Marchant Commander, but in Consideration of giving him this Receipt of our Names & the part of England we live in, and that we are ready & willing to answer our Names to Answer the Cartel of Exchange of Prisoners between the States of America and England, which is daily expected between the Congress and Great Britain for the Congress prisoners now in Great Britain he has given us our Discharge on Condition that we should Answer our Names to Dr. Franklin." This document was duly signed by owner, master, and mate of the *John;* master, mate, and three crewmen of the *Lucy;* and three crewmen of the *Ann.* For reasons left unexplained the master and mate of the *Ann,* and the seamen of the *John* were liberated without such a commitment.

That night the *Black Prince* came closer in shore and ran northeasterly along the coast of Cornwall. By late afternoon, Saturday, July 17, with the wind out of the southeast and the harbor of the little port of Padstow in plain view to windward, she intercepted three more colliers— all sloops. Two of them, the *Speedwell* and *Two Brothers,* were bound into Padstow from Swansea. The third, the *Rebecca,* was from Ilfracombe in Devon for Basset's Cove. All were ransomed. While there were a dozen men in the three sloops, Marchant elected to free unconditionally all but two of them. He extracted paroles from the master of the *Rebecca,* who signed with his mark, and his cabin boy, who did likewise.

Coasting northeastward they overtook, on Sunday morning, the brig *Union,* John Trick, master. She had come out of Padstow the day before, bound for Bristol with a cargo of oats. Brought on board, Trick objected to redeeming the brig at a price of two hundred pounds, and was told by the person he took to be the captain: "I well know this Vessell. She belongs to that old Rogue Kingdon who is well able to pay the Ransom." The speaker was Luke Ryan, who was acquainted with most of the vessels sailing out of Cornwall's north coast ports, and not Marchant, who knew nothing of the region. Ryan continued, "with a dreadful Oath," according to Trick, that he would have every vessel between King Road and Land's End. Luke already had begun to exercise some authority, it seems. Trick, perforce, agreed to the ransom, and he and his mate signed sea paroles.

In the afternoon another vessel that had left Padstow the day before was intercepted, the brig *Sea Nymph*, for Barnstaple in Devon with dry goods. She was ransomed and the *Black Prince* continued northward, aiming for the mouth of the Bristol Channel. During the night the wind swung around out of the west. They stood well off shore past jutting Hartland Point on the Devon coast, and soon were in the chops of the channel, Lundy Island under their lee. Just after dawn, with the island seven leagues off in the southeast, an inbound vessel fell afoul their path. When she failed to answer a hail, a swivel shot brought her to. She was the Spanish brig *San Joseph*, but in the custody of a prize crew. She had been taken by the Bristol letter-of-marque ship *Epervier* on July 9, on her voyage from Cadiz for Dublin. The *Epervier* had removed her crew, but had left on board the Spanish captain and two passengers, an Irish priest and a woman. A master's mate and two men had been put into her to carry her to Bristol.

Marchant took out the prize crew and with the aid of the priest, Father Bryan Murphy, who spoke Spanish, studied the brig's papers. Her cargo of wine, cochineal, and indigo was a valuable one. As a recapture more than four days in the hands of the enemy, they were entitled to one half of her. If they could prove her enemy property they would be entitled to the whole. Her original captors had considered her to be Spanish. That did not deter Marchant and/or Ryan from finding "Sufficient proof that She was an Irish Propperty," with her goods likewise consigned to Irish merchants in Dublin. They would send her to France, and Jonathan Arnold and three hands were put on board. Arnold carried a copy of Marchant's commission upon which was endorsed over the captain's signature, "I do hereby Certify that the Copy transcribed on the other Side is a true Copy Verbatim of the Original Commission I have on Board my Privateer the Black Prince Cutter, which Copy I have this Day delivered to M$^r$. Jonathan Arnold first Lieutenant of my said Privateer." The two passengers and the Spanish captain stayed in the *San Joseph*, the latter "Rejoyced to Escape an English Prison."

From where the Spanish brig had been retaken, the *Black Prince* sailed northeastward across Bristol Channel and as high up as the Mumbles near Swansea. Then she veered seaward with the Welsh coast to starboard, rounding Wermew Head, and stretching across the mouth of Carmarthen Bay toward Caldy Island at its western extremity. Two leagues off that island, Marchant hailed a small sloop, which her master, William Speer, promptly identified as the *Two Sisters*, in ballast from Minehead in Somersetshire. He was bidden to come on board, but warily asked who they were.

"Damn you, come aboard," Marchant repeated. "This is a press boat."

When Speer climbed over the bulwark, he was told she was "the Black Prince Privateer from Boston." The insistence then, and in all paroles and ransoms, upon tacking on "from Boston" was to give the Irish crew an added sense of security by pretending to hail from an American port. They took the *Two Sisters* in tow, debating whether to sink or ransom her, and proceeded around St. Gowan's

Head toward St. George's Channel. The sloop's destiny was settled within a few hours when, that Monday afternoon, five leagues east by south of Milford Haven, they overtook the brig *Dublin Trader,* Morgan Griffiths, master. She was heavily laden with a cargo of oil, copper, tin, and dry goods, and bore seventeen passengers, including a few women, all bound for Dublin from Bristol, some on business, others pleasure bent.

The *Two Sisters* provided the means of ridding themselves of the passengers. Captain Speer was told that if he would take on board fifteen of them, his ransom would be only fifty pounds. Having feared complete loss of his sloop, he accepted gladly. The passengers were transshipped, one of the ladies, a Mrs. Butler, loudly bewailing the loss of her trunks. Two passengers were held prisoners in the *Black Prince* along with Captain Griffiths and his crew of five. Prizemaster J. Bennet Negus, an Irishman who pretended to be from New Bedford, Massachusetts, took command of the *Dublin Trader,* which was kept in tow.

For two more days the *Black Prince* cruised off Milford Haven and was rewarded with a brace of prizes. On Tuesday, it was the large sloop *Charlotte,* from Cork for Bristol. Dry skins and tallow, comprising her cargo, were in no demand in France, so she was ransomed. She carried a number of passengers, who, with master, mate, and crew, signed a parole—fourteen signatories in all. Wednesday's capture was the brig *Monmouth,* a collier from Lancaster in northwestern England for Chepstow on the Severn River beyond Bristol. She was ransomed and her crew liberated with no parole exacted. The business of paroling had continued throughout the cruise in haphazard fashion. The total had reached twenty-nine with the fourteen from the *Charlotte,* and there it remained.

When the *Monmouth* was released, the privateer still had the *Dublin Trader* in tow. Shortly thereafter, she was cast off and Prizemaster Negus ordered to make the best of his way for Morlaix. For one more day the *Black Prince* remained about the Welsh coast and then turned southward for Land's End. She had eleven prisoners and eleven ransomers on board as she stood for France. Winds out of the west were at almost gale proportions as they negotiated the waters where the Bristol Channel mingles with the Atlantic. At noon, on July 23, they spoke an armed brig. She reported herself an American prize taken by a Bristol privateer. It blew too hard to send a boat on board. Suspecting her to be a packet from New York, they ordered her to keep the same course with them until the weather moderated. An English frigate—the first they had seen this cruise—made an inopportune appearance, and left the identity of the armed brig to speculation. Marchant was "Obliged to Croud what Sail the wind wou'd permit me to do to get clear of the Frigate."

In the afternoon they observed to windward a large fleet of inbound merchantmen. From the course steered, it was presumed they were headed for Liverpool. "I thought to pick up some of them," the captain reported, "but cou'd not they keeping close to their Convoy." During the night the *Black Prince* rounded Land's End, and all day Saturday stood southward across the mouth of the English Channel. A northwest wind, blowing a moderate gale, sped her on her way. At noon an English frigate was observed two leagues distant under their lee. They hauled their wind to get clear, and at eventide sighted the French coast some four leagues off to the southward. At the same time they made out the *Dublin Trader* to leeward, and bearing down upon them. She joined them before dawn, on Sunday, July 25, and that morning, "My Prize and we," Marchant dictated to Timothy Kelly, "Came to Anchor thanks providence in Morlaix Road." But the *San Joseph* had not arrived.

The *Dublin Trader* was a valuable brig. The captain advised Franklin of its worth in a report which listed eleven Englishmen brought in. Most apologetically he added, "I hope y^r Excellency knowing my Distress not having Sufficient Men to trust to Will Excuse me in not bringing more prisoners than the above." He was certain, he had done the enemy "as much Damage as was possible for me to Do." [1]

A great outcry arose throughout Cornwall, Devon, Somersetshire, and Wales as the ransomed vessels and paroled crews drifted into the various ports. Consternation seized those exposed shores from Land's End clear around to Milford Haven. Mounting rumors, exaggerated reports, wild fears were reflected in the letters that sped Londonward as the quills of men of substance scratched and splattered urgent pleas for naval aid.

First knowledge of her presence was received on July 17, when the brig *Ann*, ransomed the day before, came into Penzance. The privateer was called the *Black Prince*, said the *Ann*'s skipper, but he knew her to be an Irish smuggling wherry. She had an American commission, but her crew were all Irishmen. Then, with inaccuracy amazingly close to the truth, he pointed out that in the ransom bill the captain called himself Stephen Marchant, "but his real name is Luke Ryan." And to think, wailed a Penzance letter writer, "We have no ships of war or cruizers on the coast."

1 The second cruise of the *Black Prince* was described by Marchant to Franklin twice. The first time was in his original letter of July 25, 1779. Fearing it had miscarried, he appended a second account to a subsequent letter of August 23, 1779. Both are in Franklin Papers, APS. Supplementing his stories are the British reports, which, for this cruise, were more voluminous than for any other. Most of them are contained in a file relating to the *Black Prince* in the Public Records Office, London. The balance were accounts in London newspapers.

_In Congress_

The Delegates of the United States of New Hampshire, Massachusetts Bay, Rhode Island, Connecticut, New York, New Jersey, Pennsylvania, Delaware, Maryland, Virginia, North Carolina, South Carolina, Georgia, To all unto whom these Presents shall come Greeting — Know Ye —

That we have granted, and by these presents do grant License & Authority to Captain Stephen Marchant, commander of the Cutter called Revenge of the Burthen of one hundred & twenty Tons or thereabouts belonging to Peter Bernard and Charles Torris of Dunkirk, mounting sixteen Carriage Guns & navigated by Seventy Men, to fit out & set forth the said Cutter in a Warlike manner, & by & with the said Cutter, & the Crews thereof ... by Force of Arms to attack, subdue, & take all Ships of War employed against the United States & also to attack, seize, & take all Ships or other Vessels whatsoever carrying Soldiers, Arms, Gunpowder, Ammunition, Provisions or any Contraband Goods, to any of the British Armies or Ships of War employed against the United States, & also to attack, seize, & take all other Vessels belonging to the Inhabitants of Great Britain, or to any Subject or Subjects thereof with their tackle Apparel, Furniture, & Ladings on the high Seas, or between high or low Water Marks; the Ships or Vessels together with their Cargo belonging to any Inhabitant or Inhabitants of Bermuda, Providence, & the Bahama Islands, & such other Ships & Vessels bringing Arms with intent to ... & reside within any of the United States to pass unmolested, the Commander thereof permitting a Peaceable Search, and giving ... information of the Contents of the Ladings, & Destination of the Voyage ... & the said Ships, or Vessels so apprehended as aforesaid, & Prizes taken to carry into any Port, or Harbour, within the Dominions of any Neutral State willing to admit the same, or into any ... then the said United States, in order that the Courts to there instituted to hear, & determine Causes, Civil, & Maritime may ... and in due Form to condemn the said Captures, if they be adjudged Lawful Prize, or otherwise according to the usage ... the Port, or in the State where the same shall be carried, the said Peter Bernard and Charles Torris having given Bond ... that nothing be done by the said Captain Stephen Marchant & any of his Officers, Marines, or Company thereof contrary to, or inconsistent with the Usage, & Customs of Nations, & that he shall not commit or carry any of the Premises, & Authorities contained in this Commission, & we will & require all our Officers whatsoever in the Service of the United States to give succour, & Assistance unto the said Captain Stephen Marchant in the Premises. This Commission shall continue in Force until the Congress shall Order the Contrary —

Dated at Philadelphia October the 8th 1777

Signed Charles Thomson Secy.
Signed John Hancock President —

By Order of the Congress
Signed B. Franklin
Minister of the United States at the
Court of France —

This Commission is delivered by to Captain Marchant at Paris May 1st, 79

COPY OF FRANKLIN'S COMMISSION TO MARCHANT

That same thought dismayed all the principal inhabitants of Padstow a day later, when "A Privateer of 14 Guns besides Swivells called the Black Prince and painted black appeared off this Harbour & in the Course of 24 Hours took 13 Vessells of different Burdens." Sixteen respectable gentlemen, including the collector, the controller of the port, a notary, the vicar and one of His Majesty's principal justices of the peace, signed two appeals for help. One was to Molyneux Shuldham, admiral commanding at Plymouth; the other to Philip Stephens, Secretary of the Admiralty. They wanted immediate assistance, "this Coast being totally defenceless there not being one Kings Ship Stationed between Bristol and the Lands End to our Knowledge."

One of the merchants was convinced that the *Black Prince* was part and parcel of a nest of smugglers at Newquay, a remote port about midway between Padstow and St. Ives. "We are all in vast allarm here for two Nights the Soldiers have been under Arms," he told a friend in Falmouth, who had influence with their Lordships of the Admiralty, and who added his voice with a plea for a force to be sent "into the North Channel sufficient to protect it against these daring Pirates."

The "vast allarm" moved on northward. At Tapley, near Bideford, the collector of the port advised Philip Stephens that "the Privateer carried 16 Guns with many Swivels, and about Ninety Men, mostly Irish." She had just taken and ransomed six vessels "within sight of this House, between this & the Island of Lundy," he wrote, and the coast was totally defenceless, "both by Sea and Land." From nearby Hartland, a merchant informed Stephens, "I have been in Trade above 50 years and never remembered Such an insult to this Coast before." The armament of the *Black Prince* had become highly magnified. By now she mounted twenty 4-pounders, and twenty-one swivels, and had a consort, a ship of twenty-four 6- and 9-pounders. There was general agreement that the crew was mostly Irish. Ransomers on board were estimated at anywhere from seven to seventeen.

The sloop *John* arrived at Bristol on July 20, and two days later came word of the capture of the *Dublin Trader*. The only government vessel in port was the *Fanny*, a tender carrying about one hundred recruits, mostly victims of a press gang. She was too lightly armed to send out after the privateer. The captain of the port applied to the owners of a sixteen-gun privateer lying unmanned in the harbor. They put a crew on board and agreed to send her out with the tender. By the time they could get to sea, the *Black Prince* was beyond reach.

From Swansea on July 22, two of His Majesty's humble servants forwarded some affidavits to London. The privateer was a pirate that "was run away from Dublin River and is maned with Several Fellows that broke out of Dublin Goal and there fore are a desperate Crew having the Halter about their necks." She had been within a few leagues of Swansea and, if fifty or sixty of these ruffians should land in the night, "they might burn the Town before any Force could be collected to oppose them."

That day, too, the deputy militia lieutenant for the town and county of Haverfordwest, in the Welsh district of Pembroke, became vastly disturbed by the reports from Swansea. There was imperative need, he informed Philip Stephens, to remove from Pembroke Castle some 200 American and French prisoners. Pembroke was not more than six miles from Milford harbor and a landing party from the privateer could liberate the prisoners with ease. He had called for the Breckworthshire militia, but they were too far off to be of any assistance.

The climax came on July 23, when the Spanish brig *San Joseph*, driven by adverse winds, blundered into Padstow harbor. Lieutenant Jonathan Arnold pretended to be her master and complained that he had been plundered by the *Black Prince*. But he had neglected to rehearse this story with his three men. When interrogated separately their tales did not agree. Suspicious custom officers pushed the investigation and extracted the truth from the two passengers. The lieutenant and his three hands, the Spanish captain, and the Irish priest were marched thirty-eight miles to Falmouth. Arnold wound up in Mill Prison, while the priest was liberated and the Spanish captain paroled.[2] Off to Philip Stephens went the copy of Marchant's commission, and an account of the recapture of the Spanish prize.

Letters, affidavits, protests, copies of ransom bills and of paroles had been descending upon the Secretary of the Admiralty from more west coast cities and towns than he had ever heard of. He placed each one, as it arrived, in a folder upon which he endorsed, "Letters from Sundrys giving inform<sup>n</sup> of the piratical Vessel Black Prince." Their Lordships, after reading them at their leisure, returned them to

[2] The famous Gustavus Conyngham, then a prisoner on board the *Fanny,* a tender, enroute from Pendennis Castle, Falmouth, to Mill Prison, Plymouth, supplies an interesting account of what happened to Lieutenant Arnold of the *Black Prince*. It is contained in a Naval History Society publication, *Letters and Papers Relating to the Cruises of Gustavus Conyngham,* edited by Robert Wilder Neeser (New York, 1915), page 169: "27th [July]. This day came on boarde prisoners that was taken belonging to the Black prince privateer prizemaster Jonathan Arnold . . . Jonathan Arnold and his crew was marched 38 miles chained two and two with a guard of 24 men and officers charged Bayonnets peces Loaded. A Spanish Capt. & passenger Bryan Murphy, A Clergyman Going Hom to his Native Country was marched with 2 soldiers Drawn Cutlasses all these people was most terribly used by the Natives . . . 28th . . . the priest Got his liberty, Spanish Capt. his parole, Mr. Arnold and crew closely examined . . . 3d. August . . . I have been told that Mr. Arnold is Committed to Mill prison."

Stephens. He then bound the whole neatly with a thin blue ribbon, and filed them away unacted upon and unanswered. And there they remain to this day.[3]

[3] In the many reports of the depredations of the *Black Prince,* which went from Cornwall to the Admiralty, was the persistent one that she was smuggling brandy and tea into Newquay. The Tide Surveyor for Padstow, for example, wrote that, "One of the Masters of the ransomed Sloops declares he personally knew most of the Men on board the Privateer; they were English and Irish Men (Smugglers) that a Captain Thorn commands a Cutter which smuggles on this coast from Dunkirk under an English and French Commission and acts in Concert with the above Privateer—I am persuaded the above Privateer is one of the Smugglers."

## Chapter V

# John Torris' "Unlucky Star"

John Torris was upset. More than six weeks had elapsed since the brig *Goodwill* had been sent into Morlaix. While he believed she had been condemned in Admiralty Court, she had not been sold. The porter and other perishables in her cargo were rapidly becoming a total loss. Now another prize, reputed to be worth 150,000 livres had been brought into the same port by the *Black Prince*. Her cargo, too, included many perishables. The ransom bill for the brig *Three Sisters* had been dispatched a month before to England—via the Dover-Calais packet service by the way. Instead of remitting seventy-three pounds in discharge of the bill, his London correspondent had voiced apprehension of a long delay in securing redemption, the privateer being looked upon as a pirate.

Hope for exchange of the twenty-one men taken in recaptured prizes had been blighted by word that they had been transferred from Guernsey to Penzance to be tried for piracy, because, being Irishmen, they were regarded as British subjects. Two of the three months for which the crew of the *Black Prince* had signed up had elapsed. Shortly they would be back in Dunkirk clamoring for prize money and he had none to distribute.

Altogether the merchant considered himself in a most

"distressful" situation. According to John Diot's report no
fault could be found with the Admiralty Court at Morlaix.
Its performance had been most expeditious. Its officers had
gone on board the *Goodwill*. Hatches and cabin had been
sealed. An inventory had been prepared of what could not
be so protected. Guards had been posted. The former
master and one or two hands had been interrogated; all
useful papers translated into French, and precise minutes
—a procès-verbal—drawn up. Torris' clerk had assumed
all this constituted condemnation until he applied for
permission to sell brig and cargo. Then he learned the
entire procedure had been forwarded to the Secretary
General of the Marine Department to be placed before
the Council of Prizes. Until that body's judgment was obtained, no sale would be allowed. Diot had described what
had transpired in a letter suggesting the merchant's influence be used upon M. Chardon, Procurer General for the
Council.

If M. Chardon held for John Torris the esteem the latter
had boasted of, it was not manifested by any prompt action
in the Council of Prizes. For a fortnight his solicitations
had gone unanswered. Then he was advised that, as the
*Goodwill* was not a French prize, her disposition had been
referred to the Secretary of the Marine, the Council having
"no order to Judge the American prizes." By that time
another letter had come from Diot reporting arrival of the
*Dublin Trader,* and remarking that she was undergoing
treatment similar to what had been accorded the *Goodwill*
in Admiralty Court.

That was too much to bear. On August 11, Torris drafted
an appeal to M. de Sartine. He sketched briefly, in the
present tense, his version of the exploits of the *Black Prince*
upon her first cruise: "She disables and causes an English
ketch stronger than herself to flee, and causes five English
pinks to scatter under the coast of England. She goes into

the Channel, there carries off 8 prizes in the sight of the great English fleet; Six are unfortunately taken from her at the bluffs of Morlaix, but her great tactics allows her to lead one to port, with a ransomer."

Dropping epic narration for the factual, Torris related what had happened to the *Goodwill* in Admiralty Court and subsequently. Now, after many weeks, he had learned that the Minister of Marine was the judge of American prizes. But no order had come to sell the merchandise, so it was spoiling and his partners berated him for soliciting their money in an armament investment so "useful to the state, but which falls away to pure loss to them." M. de Sartine, he was sure, would desire to "modify my misfortunes," therefore, "This cruel ruinous delay must therefore be attributed to my unlucky star!" He requested that orders be sent to Morlaix to sell the *Goodwill;* the latest prize, the *Dublin Trader,* and all future prizes the *Black Prince* "will be able to pounce upon." He asked that the Admiralty at Brest be instructed to supply the privateer with recognition signals so French frigates would not mistake her for an enemy.[1]

So much for prizes! The question of prisoners was one for Dr. Franklin's attention. Torris wrote to him of his great uneasiness over the fate of the twenty-one men retaken by the frigate *Quebec.* He recounted the dire threats in English newspapers, and the fears expressed by his London correspondent.

"Humanity & Friendship make me Shake for these Poor People," he continued, "& I haste to Communicate your Excellency these advices, that you might Take quickly, the measures your Prudence & Wisdom will direct, to put these Prisoners of War, Sworn subjects to the united states out of the reach of malice & furour of the British Court—The

1 John Torris' letter to M. de Sartine exists in a translated copy made for Franklin by Coffyn in Franklin Papers, APS.

25 a 30 English Prisoners taken by the Black Prince & landed at Morlaix, will doubtless be aw[e]full to the Ennemy, as they might Justly be made fearful of reprisails on them."

As Torris had not been informed by Franklin of the advice to Marchant, that the captured men from the *Black Prince* would have to take their turn, the merchant presumed that an immediate exchange would be made. So, he concluded with a request "to be favoured with a few Lines removing my fears & Letting me know your Success in your promised Exchange of these 21 Men."

Not content with his own efforts, the merchant enlisted Francis Coffyn's support. The latter was willing to urge action upon Franklin, although not entirely through altruism. Many Irish sailors, lured by the success of the *Black Prince,* had flocked to Dunkirk, intending to ship in her or in other privateers. The letters from London saying she was "a Sort of a pirat, navigated by a parcell of Irishmen," and that those taken in her prizes would be tried for piracy, "had struck a terror amongst them." Hence, Coffyn implored Franklin to make a strong protest to the British Court and take such other steps as would "Save the poor men from an ignominious punishment." He took this liberty, he explained, at Mr. Torris' request.[2]

Both he and the merchant concealed another reason for their unusual solicitude for the Irish prisoners in England. Success of the *Black Prince* in her first two cruises had determined Torris to give her a consort. In this he had Coffyn's warm support and belief that a second American commission might be obtained. Before any disclosures to

---

[2] In appealing to Franklin in behalf of the twenty-one men from the *Black Prince,* Francis Coffyn pointed out that the English ought to be the last to punish these Irish seamen, as no power had been more forward "in forcing the Subjects of nations with which they are at war to enter into their Service." This letter is in Franklin Papers, APS.

the Doctor, however, they wanted to be sure of hands to man her. The Irishmen in Dunkirk were available if their fears could be allayed. Only Franklin could achieve that; could provide assurance that the lives of those already captured were not in jeopardy.

Then, too, additional funds were needed to outfit a second privateer. Before any Dunkirk merchant could be interested in such an enterprise, Torris had to prove the investment would not be delayed by governmental procrastination, and that quick profits would be realized. He also had to satisfy his brother Charles that outfitting another privateer would not be throwing good money after bad. That was why he was so concerned at the failure to convert the prize *Goodwill* into cash, or to have the *Three Sisters'* ransom redeemed. Until these problems were solved, he questioned the wisdom of applying for a new American commission. Coffyn agreed that the plan should not yet be communicated to Franklin.

Two definite steps were taken. The new privateer was to be called the *Black Princess,* and Edward Macatter was selected to command her, Ryan having strongly recommended his able lieutenant. A letter went to Morlaix recalling Macatter from the *Black Prince.*

John Torris' "unlucky star" remained, however, in ascendancy. More than two weeks elapsed after the appeal to M. de Sartine to order sale of the two prizes with no reply. In the interim the merchant had been advised that final approval of Admiralty Court findings upon American prizes must come, not from the Minister of Marine, but from the American Minister Plenipotentiary. Franklin had not answered his plea in behalf of the twenty-one Irishmen threatened with death in England, so what use was there in writing again to him? Yet ruin confronted Torris. A large capital outlay had been required to purchase the

*Black Princess.* More money was needed to outfit her. And he shuddered at thoughts of the demands he would have to face when the crew of the *Black Prince* returned to Dunkirk. He was at his wit's end, and almost at his financial end as well.

"I am in despair and do not know which way to turn," he wailed to Francis Coffyn. "You have had the kindness, Sir, of applying for the obtaining of this American Commission for me, my conduct and the privateer's have given you satisfaction, and you have always assured me, so long as the reports were favorable, that we will always have some of the execution of His Excellency M^r. Franklin. You are his agent in our city. I beg you with the greatest urgency to forward to him our complaints and the entire picture of the sad and grievous situation in which I have the misfortune of finding myself with the inconceivable delays which arise in the condemnation of prizes."

Torris' predicament enlisted Coffyn's best efforts. The agent was sure a misunderstanding existed somewhere to account for neglect of the merchant's requests. He recommended that all facts, including purchase of the second privateer, now be laid before Franklin, and that a commission be requested for the *Black Princess.* The desperate merchant was willing to agree to anything proposed.

Francis Coffyn's ensuing letter to Franklin, on August 30, began with a chronicle of events: instructions given Marchant to address his prizes to French Admiralty Courts; arrival at Morlaix in June of the *Goodwill* and hostage for the ransomed *Three Sisters,* followed a month later by the *Dublin Trader* and hostages for eleven more vessels; examination of prizes and ransomers by officers of the Admiralty, the procedure being the same as used for French prizes; papers duly sent to the Council of Prizes for formal condemnation; advice that the Council had no authority

over American prizes and had forwarded the papers to
M. de Sartine; Torris' letter to the latter which had not
been acknowledged; and, finally, the report given the merchant that Franklin alone had the power to act. Failure to
condemn, Coffyn pointed out, had had an adverse effect
upon redemption of ransomed vessels. Owners in England
were unwilling to discharge the bonds and redeem the
hostages until proper condemnation pronounced them lawful prizes. It had become imperative that prize procedure
should be brought into a regular channel so that "great
interruption to the Enemy's Trade" might continue. And
apparently the responsibility for bringing it all into a
regular channel rested with no one else but Franklin himself.

Then Coffyn disclosed the plans for a consort. Successes
of the *Black Prince* had determined her proprietors, he
wrote, "to fitt out an other Cutter of 60 feet keel & 20 feet
beam mounting 16 three pounders 24 swivels & Small arms
with 65 men all Americans & Irish under the command of
Cap$^n$ Edward Marcartor [Macatter] of Boston; this Cutter
will be called the black Princess, and is intended to cruise
in Company with the black Prince. The owners have again
apply'd to me, to request your Excellency to grant them a
Commission,   if your Excellency thinks proper to comply
with this request, I shall conform to your Excellency's orders and intentions, respecting the instructions and oaths
of allegiance to the united states to be taken by Cap$^n$.
Macarter his officers & Crew . . . if these two privateers
cruize together as intended, I hope they'll be able to keep
all their prisoners on board, which the former did not do
on account of the smallness of his vessell."

A postscript conclusion was a gentle reminder to Dr.
Franklin that he did not acknowledge letters as he should:
"M$^r$. Torris also requested me to Send the Copy of a letter

he wrote your Excellency on the 9<sup>th</sup>. ins<sup>t</sup>. which he appre-
hends miscarry'd." [3]

[3] Had Franklin acknowledged all of the letters that arrived for him
at Passy, he would have had to spend every waking moment with his
correspondence. His policy seems to have been to defer reply to letters
to which he could give no order, direction, explanation, or suggestion.
A case in point is that of Jean Rousseaux, a Frenchman who had been
captured in the Continental brig *Lexington* and escaped from England.
He wrote nine letters to Franklin between January, 1779, and September,
1783, in each begging for advances on wages or prize money, which the
Doctor had no authorization to pay. After receipt of the fourth appeal,
Franklin wrote Rousseaux that "the Business of selling Prizes, distributing
the Shares and paying Wages has never been in my hands." The subse-
quent letters from the Frenchman he ignored. Eight of these letters are in
Franklin Papers, APS, including the one upon which Franklin endorsed
his reply. The ninth Rousseaux letter is in the Benjamin Franklin Papers,
University of Pennsylvania Library, Philadelphia.

## CHAPTER VI

# The Third Cruise— Toward Ireland

SOME OF THE IRISHMEN "struck with terror" in Dunkirk would have been welcome on board the *Black Prince* at Morlaix. Six of the eleven prisoners brought in, including two of the British prize crew removed from the *San Joseph,* had engaged to serve rather than be sent to a French prison. As word had been received of the recapture of that Spanish brig, Marchant merely had traded a lieutenant and three stout seamen for a half-dozen hands whose enforced loyalty was of dubious worth. While they had been cruising, the second cartel, with Americans from Forton Prison, had arrived in the Loire River below Nantes. These repatriated men either had signed up with Jones's squadron at L'Orient, with a privateer at St. Nazaire, or had taken passage homeward. No additions to the crew of the *Black Prince* had been obtained from the cartel. She was still woefully undermanned.

Marchant had not endeared himself to John Diot while the privateer was being made ready for another cruise. He had ignored Torris' agent upon arrival by sending directly to Franklin the paroles of all prisoners released at sea. The five prisoners destined for Morlaix jail, he had herded off

without furnishing Diot with their names, or without iden-
tifying the six retained. The clerk's resentment could only
smolder and be reflected in his report to the Doctor that
the paroles "Capt^n. Marchant took on himself to forward
to your Excellency, without acquainting the owners of the
Vessell, the Commissary, or the Admiralty of it."

One of the six held on board the cutter was John Mc-
Craken, a Bristol shopkeeper and a passenger from the
*Dublin Trader*. As a middle-aged tradesman without sea-
faring experience was no acquisition, the captain recon-
sidered and gave him his liberty with permission to return
home. Before departure in a neutral Dutch ship, McCraken
wrote to Franklin, that "the Pleasure I hav in Addersing
your Excelency over balances any disapointment I have
met with in being Stopt alittle in my Journey, not only as
you are apublick Agent for American affairs (to which I
have always been afriend) but also for your Verry Phila-
siphical discourses Some of which I have read with great
pleasure."

McCraken had a great inclination to remove his family
from Bristol to Philadelphia "or Some part of the provence
of penselvenia." He had a brother and sister living there,
and had had a cousin in Philadelphia, but he "has been
dead Some years." There were difficulties to overcome before he could realize his ambition. These could be "greatly
Alivated by your Excelencys interposition and assistance
which I now make bold to request in any way that you
think most Condusive to that end." He needed permission
to re-enter France, a passport to America, and, more dif-
ficult still, agreement by his wife to emigrate. Just wherein
His Excellency's "interposition and assistance" could influence Mrs. McCraken, he did not say. Franklin could,
at least, subscribe to McCraken's postscript, which remarked, "This letter is a little Confused." [1]

[1] McCraken's letter, written at Morlaix on July 29, 1779, expressed

Confirmation of Jonathan Arnold's capture and departure of Edward Macatter brought about a reassignment of officers. Alexander Weldin became first lieutenant, and Patrick Dowlin, Thomas Connor, and J. Bennet Negus moved up in rank. The exit from the scene of the lieutenant from Connecticut reduced the number of Americans on board to one man—Stephen Marchant. Arnold's departure also served to place the captain more and more under the influence of the ubiquitous Luke Ryan. All adjustments had been completed by mid-August and the *Black Prince,* provisioned for a brief cruise but still short of hands, dropped down to the roadstead to await a favorable breeze.

In clear, pleasant weather, they weighed anchor shortly after midday on Sunday, August 15, rounded the Isle of Bas and stood northwestward. Once again the next landfall would be the southwestern tip of England. After that they would run due northward to the vicinity of Milford Haven, sweep across the entrance to St. George's Channel towards Ireland, and return to the westward of the Isles of Scilly, terminating the cruise in Brest rather than Morlaix. British frigates, fearing the combined fleets of France and Spain, would not be much in evidence west of Ushant. Just before the *Black Prince* sailed, the British Grand Fleet had been reported at anchor off Plymouth. It would not likely be under way until they had passed beyond Land's End.

Some dozen leagues south of Lizard Point they fell in with a large ship. She proved to be a Dane, which, more than two years before, had sailed from the island of St. Thomas in the West Indies for Amsterdam with a cargo of sugar and tobacco. She had been intercepted by a British revenue cutter off the south coast of Ireland. Suspecting she

---

the hope that Franklin would "Excuse any defects as I was not willing to miss the oppertunity of writing to your Excellency." The letter is in Franklin Papers, APS.

intended to smuggle her cargo into a nearby port, the cutter had carried her into Dingle Bay on the Irish west coast. For months and months thereafter litigation continued over her. At last, "with Great Cost to the Revenue," she had been cleared and permitted to resume her much-delayed voyage. Still suspicious, the British customs had placed two officers from Dingle on board to make sure she paused not on her way. Finding no excuse to prolong the Dane's homeward journey, Marchant removed the "two English Subjects as prisoners," and wished her bon voyage. With what delight his crew of Irish smugglers clapped a pair of British revenue officers in irons can be left to the imagination.

Next day, just beneath Land's End, they took and ransomed the whaling brig *Reward*. She had been fishing off the Western (Azores) Islands, and was returning to London with a hold full of whale oil. That afternoon, having rounded Cape Cornwall and running due northward, they intercepted in quick succession the brig *Diligence* and sloop *Friend's Adventure*. Both were from Basset's Cove: the former laden with wine (a good smuggling vintage, no doubt), bound for Swansea; the latter, in ballast, proceeding for Barry in Wales. Both were ransomed.[2]

During the night they veered northwest, approaching the Irish coast in the latitude of Youghal in county Cork. On Thursday morning, August 19, a few leagues south of Waterford harbor, they happened upon three colliers wending their heavy-ladened way from Minehead in Somerset-

[2] "It is a sad thing there is no ships of war to protect our trade," reads a letter of August 21, 1779, from Swansea, which tells also of the capture of the brig *Diligence*. "Yesterday a man with one arm was taken up on suspicion of being a Spy in this town, and examined before several of our magistrates. Some say he had been on board the Black Prince; but whether he has or not, it is certain that many Englishmen are on board her . . . There is an express gone from here to Milford to apprise the Transports and colliers lying there (which are about 100) of the Black Prince being out." London *Chronicle*, September 2–4, 1779.

shire, for Cork. They were the brig *Blossom* and the sloops *Resolution* and *Matthew & Sally*. Three more ransoms were exacted and three more hostages came on board. A few hours later the sloop *Betsey*, carrying pork from Bideford to Youghal, was boarded off Ardmore Head, some ten miles due east of her destination. Marchant told her master they had just ransomed the colliers, and, as his vessel "was exceedingly deep," would release her in the same manner. So they did, "after plundering him of several valuable Articles."

Hard gales were battled for the ensuing twenty-four hours. At noon on Friday, three leagues south of Waterford, they fell in with a British tender. She was heavily armed—fourteen 9-pounders, as was later learned—and showed a disposition to fight. The *Black Prince* came up and gave her a gun and she responded in kind. Several broadsides were exchanged with no material damage done either combatant. The privateer had had her storm jib set and maneuvered so badly that Ryan recommended to Marchant that they draw off and change jibs. Whereupon the tender, having lost interest in further conflict, made all sail for port. With the cutter again in trim, they overhauled her but at the expense of a sprung bowsprit. They again drew abreast and poured five broadsides into her. Response was feeble. Pursuit had carried them clear into Waterford's broad outer harbor, with Tower Hook light on their lee quarter. They dared continue no farther. On the way out to sea they spoke a fisherman who identified their opponent as the armed tender *Spry*. He also told them she had two hundred men on board; a figure which Marchant's report subsequently doubled.

Still cruising near Hook Head, a final prize was taken; another collier, the ship *Southam*, from Whitehaven in northwestern England, for Waterford. Like the others, she was ransomed. The individual amounts represented by the

eight hostages on board were not recorded, but the total
reached £2,125. Other than the two revenue officers removed from the Danish ship, there were no prisoners. Not
a man had been taken out of the prizes, save, of course, a
ransomer apiece. The reasons given were lack of room and
too many untrustworthy crew members. That was no excuse for obtaining paroles from only three of the thirty or
more in the eight ransomed vessels. No explanation for this
was ever forthcoming to Dr. Franklin.

The weakened bowsprit broke late in the afternoon of
the same day they had fought the *Spry* and taken the
*Southam*. That put an end to the cruise. Under trysail, fore-
sail, and stern jib, they steered south by east for the coast
of France. Favored by hazy weather on August 21, they
passed undetected through the British Grand Fleet some
hundred miles to leeward of the Isles of Scilly. Two morn-
ings later, nine days after departure from Morlaix, the
*Black Prince* sailed into Brest harbor.

"I am now arrived Safe in this harbour after a Short
Cruize which however has proved pretty successful"; thus
Marchant dictated to Timothy Kelly on August 23, beginning his report to Franklin. His account of what happened
was transmitted with all due modesty. He was a bit per-
turbed because only one letter had been received from the
Doctor since leaving Dunkirk in June. This had given him
"great Trouble for fear of Miscarriage," and, "as I Rec^d no
Answer from y^r Excellency makes me Suspitious you have
Not Rec^d my letters. We are almost Ready for Sea, have
got a New Boltsprit."

The "boltsprit," as Kelly spelled it, was obtained from
the King's dockyard through the kindness of the intendant
of Brest, who, Marchant boasted, "is much my friend."
With it in place, the captain bragged to John Torris he
would "do all that Lays in my power to render this Cruise
Both Glorious & Advantageous to you and all owners."

One of those owners shortly would prick the Marchant self-esteem, but, as they neared departure time, the captain strutted considerably over his successes—twenty-nine prizes, including a recapture, in the space of two months and eleven days! [3]

[3] Arrival of the *Black Prince* at Brest was duly reported in the London papers in mid-September. "Paris, September 4. The American privateer the Black Prince is put into Brest to replace her bowsprit which was broken in an engagement. In the space of three months and 11 days, this privateer, mounting 16 guns, and commanded by Capt. Marchant, has made 27 prizes, 12 of which she ransomed." London *Chronicle*, September 11–14, 1779. Marchant's report of the cruise is in Franklin Papers, APS.

## CHAPTER VII

# Dr. Benjamin Franklin, Judge of the Admiralty

IT REQUIRED AN EXPERT bookkeeper, which Benjamin Franklin was not, to maintain the record of British prisoners available for exchange. He was never quite sure of the number at his disposal. Before the first cartel, he had written David Hartley that he had about three hundred in custody. When the second arrived, he was sure more than two hundred were still on hand. Advices from Morlaix, Brest, and L'Orient punctured his optimism. His agents might be able to scrape together seventy to send back in the second cartel but no more. Prisoners had a disconcerting habit of disappearing, either by death, escape, or signing up with their captors to avoid the miseries of a French jail. A case in point was the *Black Prince*. Of thirty-two prisoners brought in from the first two cruises, eighteen had joined that privateer.

Even the twenty-nine paroles taken at sea and sent to Franklin by Stephen Marchant would scarce bring the total to one hundred—the number the British required for a cartel. Nor had he any assurance such paroles would be honored. He had intended to write to Hartley on that subject. Somehow or other in the press of business it had slipped his mind. It was recalled by John Torris' letter of August 9 with its outpouring of fears for the men of the *Black Prince* who were to be tried for piracy at Penzance, and also by Francis Coffyn's supporting plea that Franklin protest strongly against British cruelty to such prisoners.

The urgency of the appeal sent the Doctor promptly to his escritoire, where his quill fashioned one of the strongest letters he had ever addressed to his old friend Hartley on the subject of prisoners. Merchants at Nantes had urged him to send the second cartel back empty, he wrote, giving her master a sheaf of paroles taken at sea instead of Britishers. He had not agreed to that, but had ordered the agent at Nantes to collect all the enemy prisoners to be found in French jails and taken by American vessels of war, and to send sea paroles only if the number did not equal the number of Americans received in the cartel.

"I chose this method," he told Hartley, "partly in Compassion to so many poor Men who have been long confin'd here, partly from gratitude for the Charities our People have receiv'd in England, and farther to show my Confidence in the honour of your board of Commissioners, who by what they have already done, have convinced me of their humanity, and persuaded me, that this mode of dismissing Prisoners almost as soon as taken, will as it tends to diminish so far the Calamities of War, receive Encouragement from them by their ordering Compliance with the Terms Stipulated."

Having thus indited a subtle appeal to the sensibilities of the members of the Board of Sick and Hurt, he turned from paroles at sea to the subject of those men of the *Black Prince* taken in prizes. They had written him from Dunkirk, he informed the British Member of Parliament, that twenty-one such unfortunates were being threatened with hanging, because most of them had been born in England or Ireland.

"We have here in the french Prisons a considerable Number of Americans who have been taken in your service, and in America a much greater Number, perhaps more than a Thousand," he reminded Hartley. "If we are to put to death on each side all that are in these Circumstances, we shall have a good deal of Butchery in cold Blood, to no manner of purpose but to make us still more odious to one another, and create an eternal Enmity between our Posterities."

Letting that thought sink in by means of a pen flourish and a new paragraph, Franklin continued: "Let you and I, dear friend, oppose all such Mad Proceedings. We may do some Good. We shall at least enjoy the Pleasure of reflecting that we meant well, and that we strove to promote the Happiness of our Fellow Creatures and lessen the Miseries attendant on a state of War." [1] The letter to Hartley went off for Calais to catch the next packet to Dover. Acknowledgments of Torris' and Coffyn's letters could have gone by the same post, but did not—and for a simple reason. Franklin had filed both letters unanswered!

Hopes for more British prisoners had arisen in the Doctor's mind with the departure from L'Orient, after numerous delays, of John Paul Jones's rather formidable squadron. Franklin had directed the commodore to circle the British Isles, cruise until the end of September, and put into the Texel in Holland for further orders. About a week after learning that Jones had sailed, he received from M. de Sartine all Admiralty Court proceedings at Morlaix—the procès-verbal—upon the prizes sent in or ransomed during the first two cruises of the *Black Prince*. Why the Minister of Marine should favor him with all these voluminous papers he could not understand. How-

[1] This letter of Franklin's, one of the strongest he wrote regarding American prisoners, exists in Letter Books, 1779. It seems to have escaped the attention of biographers of Franklin and editors of his writings.

ever, they would afford entertaining reading when he had time to do so, but not now! He was content to give M. de Sartine a perfunctory acknowledgment. Then he turned the bulky bundle over to Temple and promptly dismissed them from his mind. But not for long!

Before September was a week old he was calling for the papers again. Francis Coffyn's latest letter had brought realization there was something more to do about those Admiralty Court proceedings than to read and file them. He was at a loss, however, to know just what was expected. Coffyn's request for a commission for a second privateer also gave him pause. Had the *Black Prince* brought in as many prisoners as he had hoped for, there would have been no question in his mind. He was proud of her exploits, but prizes and ransoms by no means answered his aims. She could accomplish those results as well under the French flag. The sole advantage to him of an American commission was prisoners. Unless he could be assured that more of them would be brought in, or more paroles taken at sea, he had no desire to become entangled in additional irritating disputes or involved judgments on prizes.

Acknowledging Coffyn's letter on September 8, he apologized for the delay because he had been, "and still am at a loss what to do as to the Condemnation of the Prizes you mention." Commissions given American armed vessels, he pointed out, directed them to submit prizes they carried into French ports to the judgment of the courts of that nation.

"I expected all along," he continued, "that the Admiralty Courts of france would try, and condemn or acquit Prizes. And I dont yet find that I have any Authority to try any Causes of the kind or pronounce the Condemnation you desire. But I shall endeavour to inform myself more particularly by consulting some Lawyers, &c. and will write you the Result."

Then he repeated the question he had asked Marchant six months before and which still was unanswered—why American commissions were desired. To avoid future difficulties, he wanted to know if it would not be best "for the Black Prince, and also the Princess, to take french Commissions."

Turning from Coffyn to Torris, Franklin belatedly explained he had written to England immediately after receiving the merchant's plea in behalf of the Irish prisoners.

"I do not apprehend there is any more Danger of Their lives than of any others taken in this War by the English," he wrote Torris, "for if Those Men having formerly been English Subjects is a Reason for hanging them, it is the same for hanging other American Prisoners, who have all been English Subjects, But on the contrary the British Government has agreed to a Cartel for exchanging them. If those men should be prosecuted, of which I think there is no Probability, my Correspondent in England will furnish Money for their Defence—But we have so many American Tories among our Prisoners, both in france & America that the Apprehension of Reprisals, would be sufficient to prevent the Enemy's taking so wrong a step. And I am persuaded the 21 Men will be exchanged in their Turn, those who have been longest in Prison claiming with some Justice to be first Discharg'd."

He concluded with congratulations upon the success of the *Black Prince,* but made no reference to Coffyn's request for a commission for the *Black Princess.* A decision on that would await the Dunkirk agent's reply.

Thus disposing of Torris, Franklin began inquiries as to his responsibilities regarding prizes. Perhaps he consulted a lawyer as he had proposed to do. At any rate, within ten days, he found the answer, much to his embarrassment, right in his own files.

Shortly after France had entered the war, M. de Sartine had advised the then Commissioners from the United States that difficulties regarding prizes and prisoners, which American privateers had experienced in French ports, were at an end. To conclude their troubles he had drafted fifteen regulations, which he submitted for consideration. The Commissioners—Franklin, Arthur Lee, and John Adams —had studied the regulations and suggested several modifications. These were returned to the Minister of Marine on August 13, 1778, by Lee and Adams, with a postscript stating: "Dr. Franklin concurs with us in these sentiments, but as he is absent, we are obliged to send the letter without his subscribing." M. de Sartine revised the regulations to conform, and they were published on September 27 of that year.[2]

Now, almost twelve months later, Lee and Adams were gone, but Dr. Franklin was very much present and very much chagrined as well, as he read the articles of the regulations in which he had concurred. These provided very definitely that a prize brought into a French port by an American privateer could be sold, if desired, along with its cargo, by taking certain steps.

First, the prizemaster should deliver a detailed report to the French Admiralty officers. The latter should then board the prize; seal hatches and cabins; make an inventory of the material which could not be so protected, such as lumber stowed on deck; appoint keepers or guards; interrogate some of the original crew members; impound and translate all essential papers; and prepare minutes of the proceedings—a procès-verbal.

Second, all original papers, the translated pieces and

---

[2] The correspondence between the Commissioners and M. de Sartine and the full text of the regulations of September 27, 1778, are published in Wharton (ed.) *Revolutionary Diplomatic Correspondence,* II, 647, 673, 682–689.

the procès-verbal should be sent—not to the Council of
Prizes! No! There it was, just as plain as the nose protrud-
ing beneath the good Doctor's steel-rimmed spectacles—
"to the deputies of the United States at Paris!" Finally, the
officers of the Admiralty could not authorize liquidation of
the prize "until they shall be required by the parties concerned."

While not so saying in as many words, it was implicit
in the articles that he should pronounce condemnation.
Certainly, if prizes were to be sold in France and ransomers
to be redeemed from England, there was no time to go
through the lengthy process of submitting the matter to
Congress. Upon him quite evidently had devolved the unwelcome task of acting as Judge of the Admiralty for American prizes. He took up the top document in the pile
Temple had placed before him, and groaned as he noted
the cramped French handwriting of M. Ringuin, clerk of
the Admiralty Court of Morlaix.[3] He was still plodding
through page after page of "Extracts from the Minutes of
the Register of the Admiralty of Treguyer established at
Morlaix," mentally and laboriously translating them into
English, when John Torris' reply to his September 8 letter
came to hand.

Franklin had voiced, the merchant remarked, "the ex-
pressions of Humanity." These would give comfort and
quiet the fears of the prisoners and encourage the men at
Dunkirk already enlisted for the *Black Princess*. He was
sure the Doctor would grant a commission for her to "the
Brave Macatter." Compliments about the success of the
*Black Prince* proved His Excellency's good disposition in
favor of those concerned in her, but compliments were not

[3] Even an adept French translator has difficulties in deciphering the
cramped hand of the Morlaix register of the admiralty in the documents
relating to two of the *Black Prince*'s prizes, which are in the Franklin
Papers, University of Pennsylvania Library.

enough. Owners and crew of the privateer were great sufferers for what Torris called the failure to obtain "Righteous Condamnation" of the prizes.

"The Cargoes are deperishing & Spoiling, & a great part thereof already Lost," he continued bitterly. "We are forced to advance daily fresh Sums for the use of our Privateer, & all the Concerns are recriminating on me for the armament. Let the appearances be what they will, Justice & Humanity, nay, the honnour & Interest of Both the American & French Government require immediate Satisfaction should be given, according to the Terms expressed in the Commission deliver'd by your Excellency. I do appeal to your Justice, Sir, & all my hopes & the relief of my havey [heavy] Misfortunes, are now Intirely Confin'd in it & in your Humanity."

There was so much truth in what the merchant said that Franklin could not resent the tone of the letter. At least, it concluded in a humbler vein. It spurred the Doctor to a renewed attack upon the procès-verbal, and to a letter to the Minister of Marine on September 18. He was of the opinion, he told M. de Sartine, that the prizes and ransoms brought in by the *Black Prince* were legitimate ones taken from the enemies of the United States. Therefore, he prayed that such directions be given to the Admiralty at Morlaix "as may be necessary for the advantage of the Owners of that Privateer."

To placate and explain were the purposes of the reply he then addressed to John Torris. He had expected the French courts to judge the prizes without any intervention on his part. Now that he had found it otherwise, he hoped the merchant's affairs would "soon be ended to your Satisfaction." His judgment upon prizes and ransoms he was enclosing for Torris' use, "as far as it shall be found valid." Apparently he still had doubts of the legality of any decision he might make.

Until Coffyn answered the question why American commissions were preferred to French ones, Franklin did not intend to commit himself to Torris upon the matter of the *Black Princess*. However, he mollified the merchant with the comment that if circumstances made it absolutely necessary, he would see what he could do. He was much pleased with Marchant's activity, and, as long nights were coming on and a night glass would prove useful on board a cruiser, he would like to present an excellent one to the captain. Would Torris please tell him where to send it?

Probably Temple attended to the enclosures and posted the letter. Whoever was responsible omitted from the judgments forwarded to the merchant the two most desired ones—that for the *Goodwill* and the ransomed *Three Sisters*. The mistake not only delayed prize sales a little longer for the harassed Torris, but it added to the aggravating details already involving the elderly gentleman at Passy.[4]

4 John Torris wrote to Franklin on September 23, 1779: "Your Excellency has omitted in the Judgement to relate the first prise of the Black Prince, Cap$^t$. Marchant Carried into Morlaix the 22$^d$ June Being the Sloop the Good Will from London to Cork, William Power, Master; & also the Ransom of the brig three Sisters for £ 73 St$^g$. Geo:Crooker master Geo:Hooper Ransomer now at Carlais. This Omission might make Some alteration, & I beg of your Excellency to send me an other Judgement for them p the return of Post According to the proces Verbal of the Admiralty at Morlaix." This letter is in Franklin Papers, APS, and Franklin's reply is in Letter Books, 1779.

## CHAPTER VIII

# The Fourth Cruise—
# in the Irish Sea

THE *Black Prince* sailed out of Brest about
September 4, bound for one final foray before the crew's
three months' term of enlistment expired. Stephen Marchant anticipated a brief sojourn around Land's End followed by a homeward dash up the English Channel. Such
had been his original orders—the privateer was to return
to Dunkirk by mid-September. They had rounded Ushant,
standing northward toward the Scilly Isles when he learned
otherwise.

That Marchant was so stupid as not to have sensed that
always he had been a figurehead is hard to comprehend.
Yet, apparently, until the blow fell the second morning
out, he had regarded himself as the unquestioned commander; had thought all decisions had been of his own
making, and deemed subordination of officers and men as
a natural acknowledgment of his leadership. It had led
him to displays of domineering arrogance that had engen-
dered resentment and hatred, long smoldering, but suppressed by Luke Ryan. To have so deluded Marchant and,
at the same time, hold an iron-handed control over his
unruly Irish smugglers speaks well for Luke's beguiling
influence, rare tact, and unchallenged authority.

When the long deception ended, Marchant's self-esteem collapsed. Ryan told him, with no mincing of words, that he had been allowed to consider himself the commander because by no other means could an American commission have been secured. There was no further need to carry on the masquerade. Dr. Franklin would be advised that the captain was a mere cat's-paw and a bungler, whose abilities were slight and who had been superseded during the voyage because he was incapable of controlling the crew, and lacked initiative for aggressive cruising. As the commission was in his name, he would be retained as nominal commander, signing the cutter's journal and necessary letters. But his powers would end there; Ryan would issue orders hereafter.

Marchant was content to remain on board under such humiliating conditions only because there was much at stake in the way of prize money. Nor was there any way of quitting her had he been minded to do so. He still had a semblance of authority due to his commission, without which the *Black Prince* would have been rated as a pirate. A strong and intelligent man could have made effective use of this weapon to maintain his position, but Marchant was neither. He accepted the degrading situation and carried on the fiction, hoping to retain some degree of dignity in the eyes of those unaware of his plight.

Ryan took charge without heralding the event to the crew, but all on board knew what had happened. Even the recent acquisitions—the prisoners who had joined to escape a French jail—accepted the fact that they were now "commanded by Luke Ryan, an Irishman." [1] The master

1 "Hague, Oct. 15 [1779]. We are desired to insert the following attestation taken upon oath to show how much the enemies of Great Britain endeavour by every means to set the neutral powers against this nation. 'On the 4th of Oct. a sailor who served on board the Epervier, formerly an English letter of marque, declared, that in order to get out of prison in France, he had engaged to serve on board the Black Prince, of

smuggler had not acted solely upon his own initiative. He
had been in communication with John Torris and knew
of the proposed consort. He believed, as did the merchant,
that Franklin, when he learned who was responsible for
the success of the *Black Prince,* would commission Irish
captains to her and to the *Black Princess.* He and Torris
had agreed that one of the objectives of this final cruise
would be to call at Rush and recruit more hands to complete manning of both privateers.[2]

Hence, instead of pausing around Land's End, the *Black
Prince* passed west of the Scilly Isles, continued her course
northerly through St. George's Channel, and on Wednesday, September 8, entered the Irish Sea. Her initial adventure can be recorded only through unfriendly eyes. First
is the testimony of one of her new hands, a late member of
the British prize crew taken in the *San Joseph:* "On the
8th of September they met a Danish vessel into which Capt.
Ryan fired a broadside and pillaged her." Second is confirmation from Liverpool four days later—of the pillaging,
although not of the broadside:

> Arrived here a Danish Ship, last from Dublin. On
> Wednesday last between the Skerries and Holyhead was
> boarded by a large Cutter of 18 Guns, and full of Swivels
> and Men, who plundered the Ship of several Stores, the
> People's Cloaths, took the Captain's Watch, and other-

Dunkirk, commanded by Luke Ryan, an Irishman; that on the 10th of
August they pillaged eight English coasters, and afterwards under English colours they plundered several Dutch vessels, although they had
their colours hoisted; that on the 8th of September they met a Danish
vessel, into which Capt. Ryan fired a broadside and pillaged her. This
deponent also declared, that on the 12th [*sic* 10th] of September they
met a Dutch brig which they also plundered. The deponent further
declares in the most sacred manner, that the said Luke Ryan always
hoisted English colours when he pillaged neutral vessels.' " *Public Advertiser,* October 23, 1779.

2 That Torris was familiar with Ryan's intention to depose Marchant
is evident in a letter the merchant wrote to Franklin before the *Black
Prince* returned to port, and which is referred to later. This letter is in
Franklin Papers, APS.

wise ill-treated the Crew. 'Tis thought she is the Black Prince and feared will do much mischief in this Channel.[3]

On Thursday morning, the large ship *Hopewell*—John Bell, master—laden with iron, tar, and timber from Gothenburg in Sweden, was intercepted almost in sight of her Dublin destination. Her crew was removed to the *Black Prince*. Six hands, including the prizemaster, were placed on board, and the brig ordered for Morlaix or Brest.

Cruising northeasterly after parting from the *Hopewell*, they fell in with a heavily-armed revenue cutter, the *Townsend*, which had just run a smuggler ashore on the Irish coast. She mistook the privateer for another of the same ilk, and ran close in to hail. On board the *Black Prince*, they watched the British commander step into the shrouds, trumpet in hand. Before he could raise it to his lips, the privateer "hoisted the Thirteen Stripes" and fired a broadside, with great damage to the *Townsend*'s sails and rigging. The Britisher carried eighteen guns, and her crew, after the initial surprise, served them well. A dozen broadsides were exchanged before the revenue cutter sheered off. There was no pursuit, for the *Black Prince* had been grievously hurt in her rigging, and her first lieutenant, Alexander Weldin, and three men lay dead or dying on the bloody deck.

The bodies of Weldin and the other victims of the *Townsend*'s fire were laced into sailcloth shrouds and buried at sea. Repairs were made and the *Black Prince* was in shape by afternoon to set off northward in chase of a distant sail. Towards dusk about four leagues southwest of the Isle of Man, they overhauled her, the brig *Peggy*, from Whitehaven in ballast, an old vessel and a poor sailer. Ryan found her not worth sending in, or ransoming. He

---

[3] This dispatch reported that H.M.S. *Ulysses*, of forty-four guns, was trying to get out of the harbor in pursuit, but the wind was against her. *Public Advertiser*, September 16, 1779.

Know all Men by these presents that we the undernamed Gentlemen Cap[t]ain and passengers of the Good Sloop Charlotte belonging to the port of Cork, Ireland, have been taken on the high Seas by Capt Stephen Marchant Commander of the Black Prince Privateer of Boston and is set at Liberty by signing your Names and places of abode to these presents under the following Obligation Viz. not to serve again the United States of North America untill the Cartell or Exchange of Prisoners passes between Great Britain and America for an equal Number of Americans Prisoners detained in the prisons of Great Britain. Given under our hands this 25 day July 1779

Morgan Jenkins London

Rob'd Edwards Capt. —

Henry Leake Cooper

John Hamilton

B. ô Donnaghere Cook

Louis B. fern

Bryten Phelos

W'm Hallman

Ly old Earll

John Colins

Smith Collins

Ro's X Irens

Cornelous Sullivan

Jon Books

PAROLE OF CREW AND PASSENGERS OF THE "CHARLOTTE"

removed the crew and applied a match. She burned with a glow visible as far away as the Calf of Man. The flames so lit up the surrounding sea that a sloop, from Maryport in Cumberland, bound for Dublin, spied the privateer hovering near the burning brig in time to put about and escape although several shots were fired at her.[4]

On Friday morning, still lurking in the vicinity where the *Peggy,* burned to the water's edge, had sunk in a cloud of steam, the *Black Prince* took another prize. She was the *Limont,* a small sloop from Liverpool with a cargo of pork for Larne in northern Ireland. By now Ryan had eighteen Britishers confined in the hold—the entire crews of the *Hopewell* and *Peggy*—and dared take in no more. More conscientious than Marchant had been about Franklin's desire for prisoners, he ransomed the *Limont,* but secured paroles from five members of her crew. The sixth he took on board as a hostage.

That same afternoon they boarded the Dutch brig *Industry.* No one in the *Black Prince* made mention of it, but enemy testimony, with corroboration, indicates that the British epithet of "pirate" was not without some justification. John Fitzpatrick, master of the brig, later testified under oath at Belfast "that on his passage here, about four leagues to the eastward of the North Rock, and to the northward of the bar of Strangford, he was brought to and boarded by the Black Prince cutter privateer. . . . After detaining him on board the privateer near three hours and plundering him of 10 guineas, some silver, his watch, buckles, and all his spare cloaths, finding his crew to be

4 The engagement with the *Townsend* is related largely from British sources, London *Chronicle,* September 18–21, and *Public Advertiser,* September 22, 1779. Marchant's reference to it was, "same day [September 9] fell in with a large privateer schooner of 22 guns, fought her for some time, and obliged her to sheer off, and took a sloop under her convoy, which we burnt, lost our first Lieutenant and three privates in the engagement"; *Pennsylvania Packet or General Advertiser,* Philadelphia, March 28, 1780, cited from the Boston *Independent Chronicle,* March 9, 1780.

Dutch, they sent him on board his ship again, after giving him a great deal of abusive language." Verification comes from the same seaman who had told of the encounter with the Danish vessel: "This deponent also declared that . . . they met a Dutch brig which they also plundered." As Fitzpatrick's affidavit was sworn to in Belfast on September 14, and the sailor's declaration came from Ostend on October 4, there could have been no collusion in the tale.

No more prizes were taken. On Sunday, September 12, they dropped anchor off the west side of Lambay Island. A call went to Rush for volunteers. Nine Irishmen came off in the boat with a promise of more once the news had spread along the coast.[5] Reports also came from shore that at least two British frigates—the Boston and Ulysses—were looking for them in the Irish Sea. They dared not risk remaining off Lambay Island, and further immediate cruising in that area might be hazardous. Ryan resolved to run up through the North Channel and foray "among the herring busses," as they called the small fishing vessels in the firths and lochs of Scotland. After British ardor had cooled, he would return to Lambay Island, pick up additional Rushmen, and head southward for the long run to Dunkirk.

To Marchant, boasting long afterwards of his cruises, we are indebted for the little that is known of this exploit northward. In one account he stated: "15th [September], went into the harbour of Liverpool [sic! Lismore?] in the highlands of Scotland, burnt two brigs there, fired into the town, and obliged the inhabitants to send off a supply of

5 "Dublin, September 18, 1779: Last Sunday afternoon the Black Prince privateer came to an anchor off Lambay and the same evening nine mariners from Rush entered on board her. It is thought that the daring appearance of the said privateer in this harbour has given rise to the report current yesterday, that the Dorset yacht had been captured by her on Monday. . . ." London Chronicle, September 25–28, 1779.

fresh provisions." In a more expansive mood, his other story gave some details thus:

> Being once in want of water and some refreshments on the coast of Scotland, he sent his boat to a small town, and demanded a supply, promising security to the inhabitants and their property, in case his demand was complied with. It was refused. Upon which he approached the town with his ship, and saluted it with a broadside. A white flag was immediately displayed by the inhabitants, and the Black Prince was not only supplied with water, but with cattle, sheep, poultry, and every refreshment the place could afford, and the commander chuse to receive.

Partial substantiation of the story, or at least of the burning of the brigs, is contained in a letter from Port Glasgow, Scotland, of September 25, which stated that the *Black Prince* had taken and destroyed several of "the herring busses." For the subsequent nine days, the record is silent. In that period, the privateer returned to Lambay Island, received more recruits, and proceeded, unmolested and unspoken, through St. George's Channel, around the Scilly Isles, and up the English Channel. She dropped anchor in Dunkirk Road on the afternoon of Friday, September 24. An officer went ashore, reporting to Francis Coffyn "that Since their last departure from Brest they have had but indifferent Success," and had brought in a hostage and eighteen prisoners. Only ten of the eighteen were landed. Eight preferred enforced service in the *Black Prince* to the discomforts of Dunkirk jail.

Even as the privateer rode safely at her moorings, Flemish residents of Dunkirk read with amusement that the *Black Prince,* "which had done so much Mischief on the Coast of Ireland," had been captured by the British frigate *Ulysses.* Not so amusing was the more accurate news that the *Hopewell* had been retaken off the French coast by a Jersey privateer.

Five days after the arrival of the *Black Prince,* Stephen Marchant appeared at Coffyn's office. He had a letter he wanted forwarded to Dr. Franklin—the last letter Timothy Kelly would pen for him. In it the deposed captain did his best to preserve his dignity and make it appear that more important service awaited him elsewhere.

"I take the Earliest Opportunity of Acquainting your Excellency of my Safe Arrival at Dunkirk in the Black prince, after Dangers from the Enemy and bad weather," he had dictated. "I am Just setting off to Ostend to take the command of a Frigate of 26 Guns called the Countess of Berigen, but expects in a few days to have the pleasure of Waiting upon y$^r$. Honour$^e$. Excellency at Passy with the Journal of my whole Cruize along with me. we burnt in the Last Cruize Some of the Enemy's Ships, Run others ashore the whole account of which I shall with all Expedition Carry with me to Paris as soon as I return from Ostend."

There may or may not have been a *Countess of Berigen,* but certainly Marchant scarcely would have been selected as her captain. Nor could he have expected to be, in view of his promised early visit to Paris. He surrendered his commission to Coffyn, applied to Torris for an accounting of prize money, learned settlement might take a few days, and left for Ostend. At least, he departed from Dunkirk. Within a week he was back. John Torris gladly paid him off, making advances out of his own pocket to do so. Coffyn, in turn, obliged with a letter to Franklin: "Captain Stephen Marchant having resigned the command of the Black Prince privateer will set off to morrow for Paris, with an intent to return to America . . . and request your Excellency will advise him in what manner he may proceed." [6]

A week before the return of the *Black Prince* to Dun-

[6] Marchant's final letters to Franklin and Coffyn's advice that the captain intended to return to America are in Franklin Papers, APS.

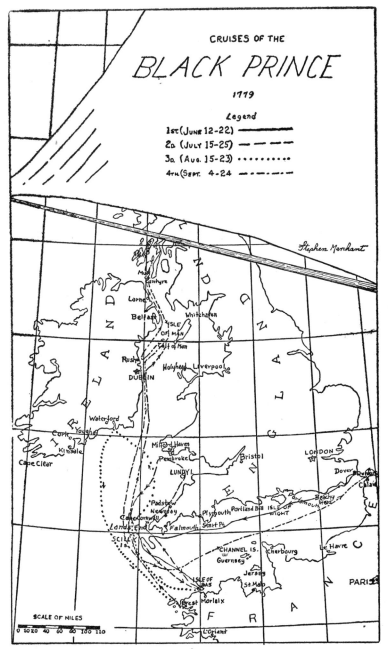

CRUISES OF THE

# BLACK PRINCE

1779

Legend

1st (June 12-22) ————
2d (July 15-25) — — — —
3d (Aug. 15-23) ············
4th (Sept. 4-24) —··—··—

Stephen Marchant

kirk, Benjamin Franklin had learned the true character of
Marchant. The Doctor unwittingly had precipitated this
disclosure by desiring to present the night glass to the
American captain. John Torris had hoped to withhold the
tale until the privateer arrived and he could have con-
ferred with Luke Ryan. The proposed gift, however, upset
his plans. He approached Franklin along a circuitous
course; extending thanks for the judgments against the
*Dublin Trader* and eleven ransoms; expressing surprise
that similar judgments against the *Goodwill* and *Three
Sisters* had been omitted; asking that the eight ransoms
from the third cruise be acted upon, and explaining that
Coffyn was supplying the reasons for wishing American
commissions.

Then he plunged into his story. The real captain of the
*Black Prince* was Luke Ryan, a part owner who had been
in her since the start of her cruise. Stephen Marchant was
but a figurehead—the "Ostensible" captain. Moreover, by
reports that had come repeatedly to Dunkirk, the American was "proved to be put [*sic*] an advanturer, neither Sea
Men Nor Soldier." All on board were tired of him and had
resolved, "at the Expiration of the 3 Months Cruise they
are engaged for, to desarm & to beg of your Excellency to
grant the deserving M${}^r$. Ryan a Commission in his own
Name, for the new armament of the Same Cutter." The
night glass, therefore, should be sent to Ryan. As the privateer was momentarily expected, it could be forwarded to
Dunkirk. The merchant's limited familiarity with the English language led him to an amusing suggestion. He believed that "a Letter of Opology from your Excellency
Joined to the Present will flatter M${}^r$ Ryan More than any
thing in the world & raise his Spirits to the Highest pitch."

Whatever surprise this astounding narrative may have
occasioned, Franklin's sole reference to it was that the
night glass would be sent in a few days. He did not even

give Torris the satisfaction of knowing to whom it was to be presented. He offered no "Opology" for the delay in forwarding judgments on the *Goodwill* and *Three Sisters,* which was the one case where an apology might have been in order. Instead, he took the merchant to task about the capture of the former. The charge that the privateer had fired upon her under English colors had created some difficulty. Torris should caution his captains "not to be guilty of the like Error again." The penalty for a second offence would be confiscation of the owners' and captain's shares. He could not send judgments on the eight most recent ransoms, as "I do not find that the Proces Verbaux relative to them have yet been Communicated to me." [7]

Thereafter, Franklin learned more about the *Black Prince*. His informant must have been Marchant, who turned up at Passy with the letter from Coffyn, and bitterness in his heart. The Doctor was told by someone, and the captain was the likely person, that the privateer had been a smuggler on the coasts of England and Ireland, had been taken and carried into Dublin, where her crew had found means to break prison, cut her out of the harbor, and escape with her to Dunkirk. Then deception had been practiced to secure her American commission.

The achievements of the *Black Prince* had been so magnificent that Franklin could find no rancor in his heart against Torris or Ryan because they had deceived him. Rather, he had a bit of admiration for the way he and his Dunkirk agent had been duped. Marchant's information, therefore, fell upon deaf ears. If anything, it enhanced Franklin's estimation of Luke Ryan.

The captain was permitted to carry on the conceit that he had left the privateer at his own volition. Franklin did

[7] Franklin learned of the true status of the *Black Prince* for the first time from Torris. The latter's letter describing it, and the Doctor's reply are in Franklin Papers, APS and Letter Books, 1779, respectively.

not indicate that he knew otherwise. The Doctor had no desire to dispel what little was left of Marchant's self-esteem. Instead, he arranged transportation for America, and the captain went down to Nantes and, after a lengthy delay, sailed for Boston. In that latter port, with no Luke Ryan present to say him nay, Marchant recited his exploits in the *Black Prince,* "that made such a noise the last year in Europe." An appreciative audience helped mightily to restore the good opinion of himself, which had been so rudely shattered that September day off Ushant.[8]

[8] Marchant sailed in the packet *Mercury,* Captain Simeon Samson, which Franklin held in port at Nantes until the end of October. She had a long winter passage of eighty-nine days to Martha's Vineyard, arriving February 16, 1780. Letter Book, Navy Board, Eastern Department, 50, Library of Congress. Marchant arrived in Boston early in March and supplied two accounts of his activity in the *Black Prince.* Both were published on March 9, 1780, in Boston newspapers: One, in the *Independent Chronicle,* was a general review of his cruises; the other, in the *Continental Journal,* was largely an incomplete list of his prizes.

## Chapter IX

# A Second Privateer
# Is Commissioned

Franklin's question, why an American commission was preferable to a French one, brought a lengthy reply from Francis Coffyn. The agent, too, had urged difficulties in disposing of prizes and ransoms as reasons for a French commission, but Torris had objections, emphatic and understandable, that had won Coffyn to his viewpoint. Thus he explained the matter:

French privateers permitted only one-third of the crew to be foreigners; whereas the *Black Prince* and *Black Princess* were to be navigated by Irish and English seamen only. Possibly a few Americans might be included. Irishmen speaking the English tongue, albeit with a brogue, could pass for Americans. If captured they would not be exposed to the punishment they would face if taken in a French privateer. This latter risk would be so great, the agent commented, that if Congress commissions were not obtained, "they would prefer to go back to Ireland notwithstanding the danger of being impress'd and sent on board an Anglish man of war." How much better that Great Britain should be deprived of resolute fellows, who, instead of becoming British tars, would turn into American seamen?

Under an American commission owners and crew shared equally in all prizes. Under a French one, one-third went to the crown. Besides this monetary objection, Irishmen were most reluctant to ship in French privateers, because "the difference of the language & customs were obstacles they can not get over." Encouragement given Irish seamen would undoubtedly bring many of their countrymen to join them, which "merits Some consideration." He reserved his most telling argument to last. If the *Black Prince* and *Black Princess* could cruise together "they will be able to bring a number of prisoners which will Serve to Exchange against the Americans now Labouring under a desagreeable captivity in England."

Coffyn disclaimed any personal advantage. He had not "the value of a shilling interest in these privateers." His sole aim was the public good, and he left it "to your Excellencys wisdom to decide wether there is, or is no inconveniency to comply with the request of the owners." These owners had flattered themselves they would obtain a commission for the *Black Princess*. Coffyn presumed this confidence had induced them to expend 100,000 livres upon her outfit—a sum "they would be Exposed to lose if it is not granted." [1]

Franklin considered the recommendations for some days. More than mere issuance of American commissions was involved. Luke Ryan was an Irish smuggler and Edward Macatter, he suspected, was of the same fraternity, and not of Boston as Coffyn had reported. There would be a few Americans on board each privateer, but certainly none in any position of responsibility. True, according to Torris, Ryan had been the real captain of the *Black Prince,* but the commission, at least, had been in the name of an Amer-

[1] Coffyn's letter of September 18, 1779, outlining the reasons why an American commission was preferable, also contains a further explanation of why Franklin was being asked to judge the prizes. It is in Franklin Papers, APS.

ican. For precedent the Doctor was aware that numerous foreigners—chiefly French and a few Germans—had been commissioned generals, colonels, majors, and captains in the Continental Army, and one Frenchman, Peter Landais, a captain in the navy. Even then Landais commanded the frigate *Alliance* in John Paul Jones's squadron. All other officers and the crew of that frigate, however, hailed from the United States, whereas, from captain to cabin boy, the personnel of the two cutters would be Irish.[2]

He could write finis to the unexpected burden which had descended upon his weary head by refusing the commissions, acting upon the remaining prize papers, and winding up once and for all the affairs of the *Black Prince*. He toyed with the idea, but, as usual, thoughts of his suffering countrymen in England tipped the scales in favor of Ryan and Macatter and their hard-bitten followers. Another exchange was under consideration: David Hartley had requested a passport for a cartel to Morlaix rather than Nantes. The enemy still held far more Americans in Forton and Mill prisons than Franklin had Englishmen in French jails, and, so far, the British Admiralty had not agreed to honor paroles at sea.

His decision was reached on September 28. No time was lost in advising Coffyn that, in compliance with his recommendation, an American commission would be issued to Macatter for the *Black Princess*. Franklin told the agent he was sorry for the trouble he had caused about the prizes. It was due to "having been little instructed as to the Part I am to act." He promised that Torris would "hereafter meet with no delay in his business from me." He demonstrated this, when, having received from M. de Sartine the papers for the eight ransoms of the third cruise, he forwarded judgments within three days.

2 The whole problem of French officers is ably discussed in Wharton (ed.), *Revolutionary Diplomatic Correspondence*, I, 397–422.

In notifying Torris that he would commission the *Black Princess* he rebuked the merchant for constantly demanding that his twenty-one Irishmen take precedence over other prisoners. "The more Prisoners you bring in," he wrote, "the Sooner their exchange will be effected." Recognition of Luke Ryan as the actual commander of the *Black Prince,* along with presentation of the night glass, Franklin conveyed on October 2, in a cordial letter condensed into a single sentence of sixty-some words:

> Being much pleased with your Activity and Bravery, in distressing the Enemy's Trade, and beating their Vessels of superior force by which you have done honour to the American flag I beg you to accept my thankful Acknowledgment together with the present of a Night Glass as a small Mark of the Esteem with which I have the honour to be, Sir, Yours &c.

The Doctor sat himself down on October 4, to draft a long overdue dispatch to Congress. It included a discussion of American prisoners. There had been a second cartel, he explained, and "Our Privateers have dismiss'd a great Number at Sea, taking their written Paroles to be given up in Exchange for so many of our People in their Gaols." Great Britain had not yet agreed to this, he admitted, but he was hopeful, as "Certainly, Humanity would find its Account in the Practice of exchanging upon Parole; as all the Horrors of Imprisonment, with the Loss of Time and Health, might be prevented by it."

For the first time he divulged to Congress his own privateering activity. "We continue to insult the Coasts of these *Lords of the Ocean* with our little Cruisers," he boasted. "A small Cutter which was fitted out as a Privateer at Dunkirk, called the *Black Prince,* Capt. Stephen Marchant, a native of Boston, has taken, ransomed, burnt and destroyed above 30 Sail of their Vessels within these 3 months." The owners were about to give this privateer a consort, and had requested a commission. Because prisoners brought in "serve to exchange our Countrymen," he was the more willing to encourage such armaments he pointed out, "tho' they occasion a good deal of Trouble."

From his privateers, he turned to the subject of John Paul Jones's squadron. It had sent in several prizes and greatly alarmed the coasts of Ireland and Scotland, he wrote. Then M. LeRay de Chaumont burst excitedly into the study, and Franklin looked up, quill poised in air. The American squadron, Chaumont cried, has had extraordinary success in the German Ocean! He calmed down to recite what he had just heard—a report that had reached Francis Coffyn via the Dover-Calais packet. Two British frigates had been captured and the greater part of their convoy destroyed. The Doctor turned back to his dispatch. "And we just now hear," he exulted, "that going North about he [Jones] fell in with a Number of Ships from the Baltic, convoy'd by a Fifty-Gun ship [*Serapis,* of 44 guns] and a 24 Gun Frigate [*Countess of Scarborough*], both of which he took after an obstinate Engagement, and forced several others ashore. This News is believ'd, but we wait the Confirmation and the Particulars."

After a few more paragraphs upon other subjects, he laid the dispatch aside. He would finish it later; after he learned more about Jones's exploit. More than three weeks elapsed before the dispatch was completed, sealed, and sent off. By then he knew that Jones was safe in the Texel with some five hundred prisoners "after one of the most obstinate and bloody Conflicts that has happened this War." [3]

When Franklin told Congress the affairs of the privateers occasioned him a good deal of trouble, he was putting it mildly. However, a few days later he conveyed much more

[3] Franklin's letters to Torris and Ryan and his long letter to Congress are in Letter Books, 1779. The latter, of October 4–28, 1779, is printed, with editing, in Wharton (ed.), *Revolutionary Diplomatic Correspondence,* III, 361–66.

emphatically to Francis Coffyn just how vexing and time consuming they were. The Dunkirk agent had received an application to parole the master and mate of one of the *Black Prince*'s prizes upon security of a hundred guineas and seventy-five guineas, respectively. This was a general French practice, Coffyn explained, and he wanted an opinion. Should he grant such paroles and, in case one was broken, should he collect the security or should it be paid to the Commissary of the Marine? The Doctor's reply was illuminating. He had no objection to the paroles or the securities, he wrote, "But as the Prisoners taken by arm'd Vessels under our Colours are, by giving me a means of exchanging so many of our Country men, some satisfaction to me for the trouble these Vessels occasion me in examining all the Proces Verbaux, making out the Judgment, answering Letters, and the Enormous Expense of Postage these Pacquets of Proces occasion the States, it seems just that the forfeiture in case of Breach of Parole should be made payable to me for the use of the united states. And if you are of the same opinion, I wish the bond or security may be drawn."

A good example of the trouble the privateers occasioned was the case of Mrs. Butler's trunks. Mrs. Butler, it may be recalled, was a passenger in the *Dublin Trader* captured during the second cruise of the *Black Prince*. When she had been set at liberty, she had left behind two trunks of clothing. In one of these, as the agitated lady remembered once she was safely ashore, was a japanned box containing some nonnegotiable bonds. Mrs. Butler had a friend, a Mr. Garvey, to whom she related her troubles and her willingness to pay fifty pounds to recover her property. Mr. Garvey thought of his own very particular friend, the elder John Holker, merchant of Rouen, who he knew was intimate with Dr. Franklin. So to the latter, via Garvey and Holker, went Mrs. Butler's tale of woe.

So trivial a matter the Doctor turned over to Temple, who wrote to John Torris. His grandfather requested that if the trunks were not already disposed of and the fifty pounds were considered as adequate redemption, would the original owner be given preference? The bonds, being of no value to any purchaser, his grandfather hoped would be returned in the original box. The Dunkirk merchant promised to notify John Diot at Morlaix to forward the bonds, and bid in the trunks as cheaply as possible. It seemed a simple transaction. Franklin heard Temple's report and advised Holker that Mrs. Butler's possessions would shortly be reclaimed. In due time the japanned box with the bonds came to hand, but Diot needed more information about the trunks. All those taken in the *Dublin Trader* had been opened and their contents advertised for sale. The agent could not pick out Mrs. Butler's belongings without a description. The Doctor wrote Holker again, suggesting this be supplied so Diot could bid them in. But the Rouen merchant had no list of the lady's goods, nor had his friend Mr. Garvey. Holker was most apologetic. He advised Garvey to handle the matter directly with Diot, and begged to be excused for "the liberty I have tooke." Franklin went not unrewarded. He received "a Quantity of Excellent apple Jelly," for which he sent "1000 Thanks to good Mad^e. Holker." [4]

"An Extraordinary Quantity of other Business," as Franklin phrased it, delayed preparation of the papers for the *Black Princess,* and a new commission for the *Black Prince.* It was just as well. Toward mid-October he was advised that ill health would keep Ryan ashore. Patrick Dowlin, the first lieutenant, was recommended to succeed him. Torris was warm in praise of Dowlin, and Ryan

[4] The correspondence with Coffyn about paroling prisoners and with John Diot, Torris, and John Holker, regarding Mrs. Butler's trunk are in Franklin Papers APS, and Letter Books, 1779.

joined in with an endorsement of him as "best Calculated in Every Respect to re, implace me." Luke had been most appreciative of the night glass and Franklin's complimentary letter. His friend, John Torris, was going to order a twenty-two-gun cutter built for him at Boulogne, to be completed in four months. By then he would be restored to health, and he asked for "a Rank in the Navy of our united Government which I will all ways uphold As My Owne Natural Government, and Loose the last Drop of My blood to Gain honnour to the American flag." Torris, too, hoped that the Doctor would obtain for Ryan "a Title in the navy of the united states." [5]

Coffyn had returned Marchant's commission suggesting that, if no blank commissions were available, it might be endorsed over to Dowlin. Both privateers, the agent wrote, were fitting out with all expedition, and should be ready for sea in two weeks. Franklin did not approve of endorsing an old document. It would be fraught with too much danger for the holder. He did expedite matters, however, and on October 15, sent Coffyn "the Commissions desired for the Black Prince and the Black Princess." "You will be so good as to fill up the Blanks properly," he continued, "and take the Bonds for the Parties, of which I send one only, not having time to copy it, but that may be done with you for the other Vessel."

Settlement with the crew for the first three months' cruise of the *Black Prince* had proven a greater headache than John Torris had imagined. Franklin's delay in condemning the *Goodwill* and *Dublin Trader* was responsible

[5] Luke Ryan's letter to Franklin of October 8, 1779, is in Franklin Papers, APS, and begins: "The Letter your Excellency did me the honnour to wright me, with the present of the Night Glass, Expressing your Satisfaction of my Conduct, in my Cruise with the Black Prince, fills me with Gratitude, and Secures for Ever my Subjection and attachments to the Government of the United States of America, and your Excellency."

for the merchant's unfortunate situation. The two vessels with their cargoes finally had been sold in November. As purchasers were allowed sixty days to make settlement, no cash for these sales would be available before the middle of January. Twelve of the ransomed vessels (those of the first two cruises) had been redeemed, but money from this source was not sufficient to reimburse the owners fully for the original outfit.

Upon the return of the *Black Prince* to Dunkirk, Torris advanced to every crew member the necessaries for their maintenance until he should be in funds to settle in full. In addition, those who re-enlisted for the next cruise under Captain Dowlin were provided with all the money they wanted. These outlays came to about 10,000 livres. Altogether, including his original advances the previous June, John Torris was out of pocket the tidy little sum of 30,000 livres, and most of the men had received more money than equaled their shares in prizes and ransoms.

This arrangement, after some argument, satisfied all hands save a group of former prisoners, who had been recruited from prizes. These refused to sign up again so their further payments were stopped. The malcontents addressed an aggrieved petition to Franklin, and, egged on by British agents in Dunkirk, threatened Torris that they would return to England and "in all probability Serve against France & America." The appeal to Franklin was returned to Coffyn with the Doctor's request that the agent or Torris "would ease me of such Troubles, I having really nothing to do with the Payment of these People."

Coffyn investigated, talked to Torris and to the ring-leader and concluded the claims were ill-grounded. He hoped Franklin would "do me the Justice to believe, that if it was in my power to hinder these people from troubling your Excellency with complaints against the owners of said privateers . . . I would not leave a Stone unturn'd to do it, as I know your Excellencys time is taken up with matters of greater Importance." Corroboration went off, too, from Patrick Dowlin and his lieutenants. They expressed their "affliction in Seeing our Worthy Friend & armateur, M<sup>r</sup>. John Torris, Injured in So gross & abusive a manner in the Bold petition Sent to your Excellency by our prisoners & foes." [6]

Arming and manning the two cutters had been retarded. Luke Ryan had decided to dispose of his interest in the *Black Prince*. She was sold under direction of the Admiralty and John Torris bought her for himself and his brother. A partnership was formed covering ownership of both cutters, which were valued at 150,000 livres. Shares were issued. Ryan took a twelfth interest, and Dowlin and Macatter a sixteenth interest each. Subscribers were numerous with John Torris making large investments for himself, his brother and others.

With these additional expenditures, the merchant overextended himself. Because of "the Situation of M<sup>r</sup>. Torris affairs," Coffyn felt obliged to take some precautions respecting the two bonds, "till matters Should be Settled on aproper footing." That happy situation was attained early in December. Coffyn secured the endorsement upon both bonds of M. Riviere, a wealthy merchant of nearby Gravelines, and who was one of the subscribers to the partner-

---

[6] Franklin was growing impatient over delays, as his letter of November 22, 1779, in Letter Books, 1779, indicates. After commenting about the complaining crew members, he concludes, "I have not heard what was done with the new Commission I sent you, or whether the Cruize of the Black Prince and Princess took place or was laid aside." The letters from Coffyn, and from the Irish officers are in Franklin Papers, APS. Coffyn concluded his letter with the statement that Jonathan Arnold, who had been taken in one of the *Black Prince's* prizes during her second cruise, had escaped from Mill Prison and had arrived at Dunkirk. According to Henry Malo, "American Privateers at Dunkerque," trans. Stewart L. Mims (Annapolis, 1911), 951, 952, Arnold subsequently commanded a French privateer, but his conduct in it in 1782 was such that no merchant "was willing to confide a vessel to him after this experience."

ship. Then, with the crews assembled before the Judge of the Admiralty, he administered the oath of allegiance to all, and delivered Dowlin and Macatter their commissions.

Only bad weather held the privateers in port. While they awaited abatement in December's storms, John Torris assured Franklin that "Nobody has any Just reason to Complain of me for the armament of the Black Prince & no Living Soul will ever have any for the new armament of the Same privateer & of the Black Princess." The wind shifted to the proper quarter on December 21. Off to Passy went the bonds, with Coffyn's notification that both privateers had sailed that morning. And he added, "I never Saw a Sett of more resolute fellows than those which compose their Crews." [7]

[7] The agreement for the joint cruise of the *Black Prince* and *Black Princess*, dated October 6, 1779, is printed in *ibid.*, 954, 955. It provided that John Torris "shall alone be charged with the plans of campaign . . . of the disposition of prizes and ransoms, of sales and all other matters pertaining thereto," and specified that he would not be compelled to seek any further authorization for expenditures than what was given him in the agreement.

## CHAPTER X

# The Joint Cruises

NOT ALL MEMBERS of the crews of the two privateers were the "resolute fellows" Coffyn had boasted of. The number of Irishmen available in Dunkirk, even with the recruits arrived from Rush, had not been adequate to man both vessels. Smugglers comprised but two-thirds of each complement. The balance were Frenchmen, whom the commissary, just before sailing, had permitted Dowlin and Macatter to sign on for a three months' cruise. They had all the appearance of seamen, but proved to be the flotsam and jetsam of the port, and would act "neither as Sailors or Soldiers."

Reports had been prevalent in Dunkirk that a fleet of better than a hundred merchantmen was lying in the Downs awaiting convoy down the English Channel. When the *Black Prince* and the *Black Princess* stuck their noses out of the roadstead in hard, blowing weather, they steered to the northeast to round the Goodwin Sands and drop down upon this fleet from the north for a bit of investigating. A British informer noted their course and reported them as "certainly destined for the North Sea," a distinct service to the privateers, who were bound instead for the usually fruitful cruising ground around Land's End.

They gained the Downs and lay there for three days undetected. This amazing feat, performed despite their tell-tale appearance, was possible because bitter December weather drove the watch on each merchantman to shelter behind bulwark or deck house, while the security of the anchorage invited laxity on board the two English cutters guarding the fleet. There could have been lush prize-taking, but no point in attempting it, as captured vessels could not have been ushered out of the Downs in the face of howling winter winds. Dowlin and Macatter secured a lot of information, however, from occasional unsuspicious masters or mates who responded to friendly hails. Thus they learned that most of the fleet was bound for the Lee-ward Islands and would be convoyed from Spithead by a formidable squadron under Admiral Rodney. The rest were London ships waiting to proceed for various ports on the west coast of England or the eastern shores of Ireland. These would be unprotected once Rodney veered south-ward to round Ushant, and would be the logical quarry to intercept along the stretch from Lizard Point to Cape Cornwall. The captains even obtained names and destina-tions of several of the more promising merchantmen, be-fore departing, with the first break in the weather, ahead of the fleet to lay in wait for their intended victims.[1]

The initial prize was none of these, but a heavily laden brig, the *James and Thomas,* Dublin for London, with a cargo of butter and salt provisions. She was taken the day after Christmas, 1779, some four miles east of the Lizard, after a hail and three 4-pound shot from the *Black Prince* brought her flag down on the run. In addition to her crew, she carried sixteen seamen and boys intended for Sheerness as part of "the complement for the Indies." Dowlin re-

[1] Rumors and reports regarding both privateers appeared in the London newspapers almost daily during January, 1780. The news that they had lain in the Downs with the British merchant fleet was con-veyed in a dispatch of January 3, which was reprinted in the *Pennsylvania Journal,* Philadelphia, on April 5, 1780.

moved all hands, including the draftees for the service of the East India Company. He manned her then with a prize crew of six, and ordered her for Morlaix.

Within twenty-four hours two more captures were made. One was a small collier, the brig *Betsey,* bound from Swansea for Penzance. She was intercepted by the *Black Prince,* and ransomed. The other was taken off Land's End by the *Black Princess;* the ship *Camden,* which had come a long way—from Memel in the Baltic—with a cargo of construction lumber destined for Liverpool. Her ailing master offered to ransom her for six thousand pounds, but was refused. Macatter took out her crew, put the usual half dozen men on board, and sent her off for France.

Two brigs, the *Ceres* from Yarmouth for Liverpool, and the *Polly,* from Cork for London, fell afoul of the privateers on December 28 about six leagues north of Land's End. Each was ransomed for one thousand guineas. Dowlin took both ransomers on board the *Black Prince.* The master of the *Camden* proving a very sick man was released and sent on board the *Ceres.* Before permitting the *Polly* to resume her voyage, her master was interrogated about "the Bristol traders to Dublin and Corke."

If Dowlin and Macatter had any intentions of cruising farther northwards toward the Bristol Channel, the idea was abandoned that night as the London ships from the Downs began to appear. First intercepted was the brig *Lively,* bound for Liverpool. The weather had been fair for the first few days on the cruising ground, but had turned boisterous. When the brig came to in response to several shots from the *Black Prince,* the sea ran too high to send a boat to her. Dowlin had to content himself by running in close, learning her name and destination, and trumpeting a command to follow him till dawn. By daybreak, off the Scilly Isles, the *Lively* was not in sight.

Better luck and milder weather favored them that day.

Four of the London merchantmen were captured between sunrise and dusk. Two were taken by the *Black Prince:* the brig *Owner's Adventure,* bound to Cork with flour, peas, and iron, and the sloop *Providence,* for Barmouth in Wales with a cargo of wool. The prizes of the *Black Princess* were the brig *Prince William,* with provisions for Dublin, and the sloop *Peter and John,* similarly laden for Waterford. To this haul, Macatter added after dark the brig *Betsey,* from Dublin for London with beef and butter, and two coasting sloops. By then the privateers had taken more vessels than they could man, and had accumulated more prisoners than they could safeguard. The two coasters —the *Samuel and John* for Milford, and the *Hereford,* destination not given—were ransomed. In the Milford-bound sloop they placed the masters of the *Peter and John* and of the *Betsey,* exacting paroles from each. Prize crews boarded the other five vessels, prizemasters being instructed to make for any port they could reach on the Brittany coast, preferably Morlaix, and to avoid sailing in company as the best means to avoid recapture. The lesson learned on the first cruise of the *Black Prince,* when a cluster of six prizes had been retaken by the *Quebec* frigate, had not been forgotten.

Discounting the brig that had slipped through their fingers, Dowlin and Macatter had been unusually successful. Seven prizes were on the way for France. Five vessels had been ransomed for about £3,000, and there were sixty-eight prisoners in their holds—forty-eight in the *Black Prince* and twenty in the *Black Princess.* Considering the number of men, largely Irish, sent off in prize crews, their complements were too reduced to continue cruising, particularly with the unreliable French hands and so many captives. They turned southward across the English Channel.

To the northward of Ushant two British frigates gave chase. Macatter steered eastward and Dowlin to the southwest. The enemy ignored the *Black Princess,* which arrived in Morlaix Road on January 6, 1780. Pursuit of the *Black Prince* continued with unabated zeal for two days and a night. Dowlin tried for Brest, but winds prevented his reaching the Passage du Pour. The frigates clung to his heels until, having rounded the whole jutting nose of Brittany, he found safety in the harbor of L'Orient.

Five of the prizes reached port before or right afterwards. The ship *Camden* came into Perros roadstead, a few leagues east of Morlaix, and proceeded to run on a rock. Eventually she was gotten off with little damage. The brig *Betsey* entered Brest harbor and upset, but was righted without loss. The others suffered no mishaps in getting in; the brig *James and Thomas* at Morlaix, the sloop *Providence* at Cherbourg, in Normandy, and the brig *Owner's Adventure* at Audierne, a small port on the Brittany coast about midway between Brest and L'Orient. Two prizes were retaken; the *Prince William,* which a British privateer intercepted and carried into Lisbon, and the *Peter and John,* whose recaptor is not apparent.[2]

Patrick Dowlin spent but a few days at L'Orient. He landed his prisoners and ransomers and took the *Black Prince* around to Brest for repairs. At Morlaix, meanwhile, Edward Macatter, who had lost a dozen men in the *Prince William* and *Peter and John,* found a welcome reinforcement of twenty-one American seamen. They had been prisoners for almost a year in Pembroke Castle in Wales. Under the leadership of Charles Collins, a midshipman in the Continental navy, they had broken out of jail, seized a small sloop and sailed her in triumph into Morlaix. There being "no Contenantle Ship as I Cold go on Bord

2 Letters from John Diot and a report of the cruise by Patrick Dowlin are in Franklin Papers, APS. Full details of two of the prizes—the *James and Thomas,* and the *Camden*—are in the copious papers comprising the minutes of the register of the Admiralty at Morlaix, in the Franklin Papers, University of Pennsylvania Library.

of," Collins wrote Franklin, "I thought proper to go on Bord yᵉ Black princess Cutter." [3]

By the end of January both privateers had been over-hauled, graved, and provisioned. Neither captain had heard from Franklin, which was not remarkable as neither had written to him. Reports upon their cruises had been left to John Diot at Morlaix, and John Torris' L'Orient agent. Dowlin got around to letter writing on January 27, from Brest:

> I hope Soon to be Ready to set to Sea and Expects and determines to do as much hurt to the Enemies of United States as I possibly can   in a day or two I Expect to join Company with the Princess at the Isle of Bas(s) where she now is, and so proceed on our Intended Cruize, If yᵉ Excellency Chuses to favour me with an Answer please to direct to Patt Dowlin Capᵗ. Black Prince at Mʳ. Clancey's Merchant in Roscow, Normʸ.

Contrary winds held the *Black Prince* in Brest harbor, so Dowlin did not reach the rendezvous until mid-February. They cleared the Isle of Bas on February 24, and next day, midway between Ushant and Land's End, met the schooner *Peter,* Thomas Byrne, master, coming out of the Channel on her way from London to Madeira with a cargo of staves and flour. She mounted six 3-pounders, but

3 Charles Collins on March 29, 1780, in a letter in Franklin Papers, APS, gave Franklin an interesting account of his experiences before joining the *Black Princess:* "I was taken the 9 of September In yᵉ yer 1778 In a Contenantle Brig Resistance mounting 18 guns William Burk[e] Capten I was In Compassity of a mid Shipman on Bord Bound with Exprest for Counde Estang . . . the 14 day I was put in Rhodisland prison with 9 pepole with me   the 22 Day I was taken out on Bord the Culloden an English 74 gun Ship . . . I was on Bord till we arive at milford haven and yᵉ 15 Day of December wee was put on Shore In pembroc prison   wile I was on Bord I was used Very Barbresly and always Intisoning me to Enter But I refused   after Being in prison 12 months and 6 days I and 20 americans Brok out of prison tuck a Small Sloop 7 miles up the River past by Sevrel firgets and tenders and Came Safe to france adter Being at Sea 3 days without watter or pervisions." See also, William Bell Clark, "The Continental Sloop *Resistance,*" *American Neptune* (Salem, January, 1954).

made no use of them. Master and hands were brought on board the *Black Prince* and a prize crew headed the *Peter* south for Morlaix.

Next day, still in the Channel, they took the large brig *Philip*, laden with sugar, cotton, and coffee, bound for London from the far-off island of St. Lucia in the West Indies. Macatter took out her crew and put in his own men to carry her also into Morlaix. They reached and hovered about their favorite cruising ground for several days and were rewarded on March 2, with a third prize, the brig *Friendship*, from Lisbon for London with a cargo of salt, fruit, and wine. She followed the *Peter* and the *Philip* for France, manned by a prize crew from the *Black Prince*. Dowlin through oversight, carelessness, or disregard of orders, did not furnish his prizemasters on board the *Peter* and the *Friendship* with any of the papers necessary to prove enemy ownership; an omission he would in time regret.

The *Black Prince* and the *Black Princess* rounded Land's End and stood northwestward toward the Irish coast. On March 5, abreast of Wexford, they took a wherry carrying fish and potatoes from Dungarvan in county Waterford for Dublin. They removed the crew—three men and a woman —helped themselves to as much of the cargo as they needed, and scuttled the vessel. After that they set a course due northward up the center of St. George's Channel, headed for the Irish Sea.

His Majesty's post office operated a fast mail and passenger service to Ireland; packets plying the sixty-odd miles between Holyhead, at the northwestern tip of Wales, and Dublin on a daily schedule. Passage in normal weather required about eight hours. Speed was a substitute for armament. The post office prided itself upon this, and boasted that since the beginning of the war no vessel on this run had been taken. The *Black Prince* and the *Black Princess*

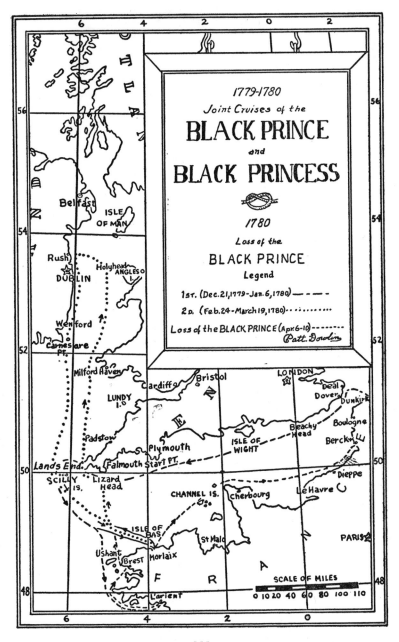

1779-1780
Joint Cruises of the
BLACK PRINCE
and
BLACK PRINCESS
1780
Loss of the
BLACK PRINCE
Legend

1st. (Dec. 21, 1779 - Jan. 6, 1780) — — —
2d. (Feb. 24 - March 19, 1780) ∙∙∙∙∙∙∙∙∙∙
Loss of the BLACK PRINCE (Apr 6-10) - - - - - -
Patt. Dowlin

proceeded to shatter this complacency by taking not just one, but two of these packets in rapid succession.

The *Hillsborough,* which had sailed from Holyhead shortly before noon on March 7 with a London mail and a few passengers, was intercepted at twilight not far off the Irish coast. Her master sank his mail bags before a boat crew from the *Black Prince,* with Patrick Dowlin in the stern sheets, came alongside. The passengers were handled none too gently by the boarders. Amid much profanity and behaving "in the most indelicate manner to the women," everybody was searched and stripped of all valuables. If Dowlin did not participate in the looting, he did not forbid it. Leaving a number of well-armed men in the *Hillsborough,* he returned to the *Black Prince,* the prizemaster being instructed to keep company with the privateers through the night.

These ex-smugglers were quite familiar with the Dublin-Holyhead schedules. They knew that about midnight another packet would sail out of Dublin. Rather than miss her in the darkness, they stood easily along eastward upon the course she would pursue, figuring she would overtake them shortly after daylight. Sure enough, she did—just about six leagues due west of Holyhead. She was the *Besborough,* with two mails and a goodly passenger list. The packet's master managed, as had the master of the *Hillsborough,* to drop his weighted mail sacks over the side. This time a lieutenant went on board with Dowlin. Passengers and crew were addressed with vivid Irish expletives. The women were recipients of some indecent remarks. All jewelry and money found its way into the pockets of the captors. According to one Edmund Dunkin, the officers, too, treated everybody in the *Besborough* "in a most Savage manner." He averred that, in a stand-and-deliver style, "Dowlin robbd me of a Gold watch value about Sixty-four Guineas whilst his Lieut. rifled my Pockets of about Ten Guineas & some Shillings & did leave me one farthing."

As neither packet carried cargo of any value, Dowlin and Macatter decided not to send them for France. On an enemy coast in a blustery March, short of provisions, and with the French hands increasingly insubordinate, the two captains determined to rid themselves of all prisoners by placing them in the packets under the usual sea paroles. Twenty-one Britishers were divided between the vessels, which were then released under ransom and ordered for Holyhead.

The packets arrived in that Welsh port that night. An alarmed postmaster dispatched an express to London, and notified his confreres all up and down the coast of the calamity that had befallen His Majesty's Irish mail service.[4] Within a week the principal inhabitants of Whitehaven had a petition to the Admiralty signed and circulating for more signatures in Workington and Maryport. It called for cutters to be sent into the Irish Sea to protect the trade, "the frigates hitherto employed being altogether inadequate to the service required of them."

Upon parting with the *Hillsborough* and the *Besborough*, the *Black Prince* and the *Black Princess* turned

4 "Holyhead, Post-Office, March 8, 1780. Sir. I am sorry to acquaint you that the Hillsborough and Besborough packet boats have been taken by the Black Prince and Princess privateers, the former of 20 carriage guns, 22 swivels, and 100 men; the other, 16 guns and 90 men. The Hillsborough left this at 11 o'clock yesterday morning, with one mail, and was taken at six o'clock in the afternoon. The Besborough, with two mails from Dublin, was taken this morning at eight o'clock, within six leagues of the Head; the three mails were sunk, and the packets being ransomed, arrived here this evening; the crews of both privateers were Irish: The name of the Captain of the Black Prince privateer is Patrick Dowlin. If wind and weather permit, I intend sending out the Hillsborough and Le Despencer, in hopes through the favour of the night, one, if not both, will be able to get over with this intelligence. I have sent an express to Mr. Todd. I should have told you the privateers have American commissions from Dunkirk. I am, Sir, your most obedient very humble servant, William Vickers. Per express [To] John Lees, Esq. . . ." London *Courant*, March 21, 1780.

westward to cruise for a few more days off Dublin. Dowlin came close to taking a third one of His Majesty's packets early the following Saturday morning. She was the *Despencer,* bringing news of the double capture. He chased her until he touched a sand bar, at the entrance to Dublin harbor, forcing him to abandon pursuit. He and Macatter ran northward to put ashore at Howth the three men and a woman from the wherry he had sunk six days earlier. Perhaps they recalled that off Howth a year before they had sent the revenue officers off in a boat from the same *Black Prince,* then known as the smuggling cutter *Friendship.* The next port of call would be at Rush for recruits. They approached that harbor late Saturday night, but the wind was high and out of the southwest, blowing them off shore, so they gave over the attempt.

It was well they did. One of the passengers of the *Hillsborough* arrived at Dublin in the *Despencer* and reported that the privateers intended for Rush to deposit some plunder and take in fresh water. The forces of His Majesty were marshalled—the Merchants Corps and detachments from the Dublin, Goldsmith, Liberty, and County Volunteers—and, nigh three hundred strong, with sixty rounds of powder and ball, set out at midnight from the Royal Exchange to surprise "these freebooters." Fourteen long, dark, and dismal miles they marched, and at daylight were within half a mile of Rush. Their leader, a justice of the peace from the courts of Dublin, halted the citizen-soldiery and "addressed them in a spirited manner." Then with bayonets fixed and cheering as they went, they stormed into the town, "but to their very great disappointment," no privateers lay in the harbor. Like that nursery-rhyme king of France, who "marched them up the hill and marched them down again," the justice of the peace led them back to Dublin, "so that in the course of seventeen hours they went through a fatiguing march of 28 miles."

And the chronicler of the event might well have added, "for nothing."

At that time, the *Black Prince* and the *Black Princess* were headed southward through St. George's Channel, homeward bound.[5] Five leagues off Tuskar, a rugged rock lying close by the Irish coast near Wexford, they boarded the brig *Nicholas,* from Cork for Liverpool, and ransomed her. With no further interruptions, they passed between the Scilly Isles and Land's End, crossed the mouth of the English Channel and, as Dowlin reported, jubilantly if not grammatically, "on the 19th. the Princess our Consort and me Came to Anchor in Morlaix Road." Their three prizes had preceded them in by better than a week.[6]

Behind in Ireland, a loud wail had arisen against the Admiralty for "paying so little attention to the trade in that part; two American corsairs have been in the Irish Sea for four months." Well, it seemed that long to the merchants of Dublin, Cork, and Waterford. And news that the Admiralty had added a frigate and two cutters to the futile search for the marauders failed to still the denunciations.[7]

[5] "Extract of a letter from Dublin, March 20 [1780]. 'Complaints are very loud in the North part of this kingdom against the Admiralty for paying so little attention to the trade in that part: the two American corsairs have been in the Irish sea four months, and yet the Thetis man of war has been the only ship stationed there: She has been hurried about other places in Scotland, and then back here. The Boston frigate and the Alarm and Pleasant cutters, have now taken that station: the Thetis is ordered home to Plymouth, but is to call at Milford to take the trade under convoy from thence.' " London *Courant,* March 28, 1780.

[6] Dowlin's two letters, one at the start and the other at the conclusion of the cruise, are in Franklin Papers, APS.

[7] The usual rumors that the *Black Prince* had been captured followed this cruise. "I have just now the pleasure of being informed, that the Black Prince privateer, which has made such havoc, and caused such fears in the coasting trade, is this morning brought into Falmouth by the Aurora frigate." Thus read a letter of March 13, 1780, from Truro, appearing in the London *Chronicle,* March 16–18, 1780. One issue later, that newspaper admitted, "The Black Prince Privateer is not taken, as mentioned in all the papers."

## Chapter XI

# *Mainly About Prisoners*

Despite five hundred British seamen brought into Holland by the squadron of John Paul Jones, despite all the prisoners sent in by the *Black Prince* in her summer cruises, despite many men liberated at sea on parole, and despite passports supplied for cartels, not one additional American had been exchanged from Forton or Mill prisons since the preceding June. That was six months before and, by the beginning of the year 1780, Benjamin Franklin might well have yielded to despair as he considered how his efforts to relieve his unfortunate countrymen had been baffled at every turn.

High hopes of exchanging them for the British crews Jones had carried into the Texel had been shattered by an Admiralty refusal to treat with him for prisoners in Holland. The enemy knew the American squadron could not remain indefinitely in a neutral port. As a heavy cordon of warships blocked the Texel, there was every chance of intercepting any vessel that might seek to bring these prisoners to France. So why exchange what they might with patience repossess? Franklin had been forced into an unwelcome concession to defeat British expectations. He had agreed with M. de Sartine that Jones's prisoners should be turned over to the French Ambassador in Holland, who

I take the earliest Opportunity of Acquainting your Excellency of my Safe Arrival at Dunkirk in the Black Prince, after Dangers both from the Enemy and bad weather, we are safe arrived and hath ten prisoners in Dunkirk Goal. I am just setting off to Ostend to take the Command of a Frigate of 26 Guns called the Countess of Beaujin, but expects in a few days to have the pleasure of Waiting upon your Honoured Excellency at Paris with the Journal of my whole Cruize along with me we burnt in the Last Cruize some of the Enemys Ships, run others ashore the whole Account of which I shall with all Expedition carry with me to Paris as soon as I return from Ostend, my kind Complts. long your Excellencies Nephew and the Rest of the American Gentlemen at Paris I remain with all Duty your Excellencies most

Obedient Humble
Servt.
Stephen Marchant

MARCHANT REPORTS UPON "THE LAST CRUIZE"

Honord Sir                    L'Orient 19th Jan. 1780

42

The privateen Sloop Black prince under
American Colours, put into this harbour some
days since: she sailed last from Dunkirque, and
(during) a Cruise of eighteen days in the English :
Channel, (in consort with the Black princess) she
made several captures and deposited Forty eight
prisoners here. we take the liberty of mentioning
this circumstance to you, that in case those
prisoners are to be looked on as the property
of the united States, you may take such order
therein, as will distinguish them from those of
this Kingdom

        we have the honor to be with respect
        Honord Sir    Your most ob't serv.
                      Courlade & Maylan

THE "BLACK PRINCE" LANDS FORTY-EIGHT PRISONERS AT L'ORIENT

would exchange them from the Texel for Frenchmen in captivity in England.[1] In return, an equal number of British prisoners taken by the French and in French prisons would be allocated to the Doctor to redeem for his countrymen.

Thus matters stood when Franklin received from David Hartley a charming but over-optimistic assurance that the Admiralty had been prevailed upon to dispense with the tedious mode of exchanging but one hundred prisoners at a time. To confirm this, Hartley enclosed copy of a letter from the Commissioners of Sick and Hurt. It conveyed a comforting statement that the Commissioners had "their Lordships directions for Making an Exchange of all the American prisoners in England." It also contained some instructions to accomplish this desirable end, which the guileless Hartley either overlooked or misunderstood.

Fortunately another Englishman, who had the same humane disposition, but a more practical viewpoint, corrected Hartley's oversight, and avoided complications and confusions for Franklin. He was William Hodgson, a London merchant who had been one of the Doctor's friends in prewar England. Hodgson had been active in ameliorating the distress of unfortunate Americans from the moment that grim Mill Prison had been opened, and had been instrumental in launching and maintaining the charitable subscription to supply them with clothing and other necessaries. His letter, penned a week after Hartley's announcement, disclosed that the Commissioners had no intention of sending any more men in a cartel to Morlaix than Franklin had prisoners to return for them. Hodgson had frequent occasion to attend the Commissioners, he explained, and found them "disposed to act as fairly & openly as can

[1] In Papers of the Continental Congress, 193, 151, National Archives, Washington, is a letter of December 6, 1779, from Franklin to Jones, telling of this arrangement.

well be expected." He opined that many unhappy Americans might have been liberated long since had a proper understanding existed between the Commissioners and Franklin.[2] Maybe so, but the editor of an anti-administration London newspaper probably came nearer the truth with the comment that "the real cause of the detention in gaol of these unhappy brethren (many of whom have been three years in prison) is the fear of their getting on board Paul Jones squadron."

Regardless of reasons, the delay to Franklin was infuriating. He wrote Hodgson that while the Commissioners of Sick and Hurt might do what was humane, just, and honorable, he had no such good opinion of their Lordships of the Admiralty, "from whom Mr. Hartley has never been able to get a yes or a no on the plain question whether the written paroles or engagements of English prisoners set at liberty by our cruisers were to be complied with." From Hodgson's letter, the Doctor inferred that the Admiralty had determined such paroles were not to be honored, so he told the merchant that he would order his captains to issue no more of them, but to bring in all prisoners. "How much human misery might be saved by continuing the other method!" he exclaimed. "I thought confidence, if it had not begot confidence would at least have produced justice, but I was mistaken."

In accounting to Hodgson for the prisoners in his custody he was, of necessity, quite vague. He still had no report upon the number held in Spain. News of the sixty or more brought into L'Orient and Morlaix by the *Black Prince* and the *Black Princess* had just been received. All

2 William Hodgson's correspondence with Franklin opened with this letter, dated November 23, 1779, and is in Franklin Papers, APS. Through careless transcribing the two Hales, in *Franklin in France*, attributed two letters to Hodgson in October, 1779, which were, instead, written by David Hartley.

told, he could figure on close to a hundred available for exchange.

He gave assurances to David Hartley on February 2, that he could exchange man for man the number in two more cartels by adding those taken by the French "with whom we have an account since the exchange in Holland of those we carried in there." In the belief that the exchange was now fully set in motion, Franklin acceded to a request from M. de Sartine on February 13, and issued an order for the British prisoners at L'Orient and Morlaix to be placed on board the *Happy Return,* a cartel ship which had brough French prisoners from England. The Doctor was quite willing to oblige, as Hodgson had just advised him that a cartel was about to sail from Plymouth with one hundred Americans on board.

Under arrangements made in Holland, Franklin could anticipate quick release of all those in Forton and Mill prisons, or so he informed his London merchant friend. "The English prisoners to exchange for them will be ready at Morlaix," he wrote on February 26, "and . . . if the whole number of American prisoners in England are sent over without further delay an equal number of English prisoners here, whether taken by the Americans or the French will be immediately returned for them."

Meantime he dispatched instructions to his Irish captains regarding paroles at sea. Writing to Patrick Dowlin, "at M<sup>r</sup>. Clancey's in Roscow," and intending the order for Edward Macatter as well, he extended congratulations upon the successful December-January cruise, and then launched into his directive:

> The prisoners you have brought in will soon procure us the liberty of as many of our countrymen, who have long been confined in the jails of Great Britain. It is therefore an essential piece of service to the United States; and

as the English pay no regard to the written paroles formerly taken from the men who were prisoners to the Black Prince and set at liberty, I think it right that you should trust no more to the honour of that nation, which has refused to return us a single man on account of those paroles . . . and for the future I desire that you would secure your prisoners as well as you can, and lodge them in French or Spanish jails, by which means you will have the satisfaction of relieving many poor captives and recommending yourself to the favor of Congress.[3]

At Dunkirk Luke Ryan, fully recovered, now commanded a privateer of one hundred and fifty tons burden. John Torris had abandoned the idea of having a vessel built at Boulogne. Instead he had purchased "a Fine Large Cutter," mounting eighteen 6-pounders and twenty swivels. "I shall put on board 100 Stout Americans, Irish & Strangers," he had reported, "the most of which are allready Listed with M[r]. Ryan. We Shall give her Name the Fearnot. I Petition your Excellency to grant me forthwith, favour of Cap[n]. Ryan an American Commission for the Cutter."

Luke Ryan had joined his pleas to that of the merchant. Nothing in the world would give him more pleasure, he had asserted, than a fresh opportunity to distinguish himself in the cause he had embraced and to render further service to the nation to which he had sworn allegiance. He had been offered a French commission, but had spurned it, because he would not serve otherwise than under American colors. "I persuade myself Your Excellency will approve of my refusal and Inclinations," he had continued, "and will grant me forthwith the Commission from Congress I Do sollicit for the Cutter privateer the fearnot under My Command . . . I am bold to assure your Excellency that my Cutter manned as she is, may do

3 All of Franklin's letters to Hartley, Hodgson, and Dowlin, quoted in this chapter are in Letter Books, 1780, in the Library of Congress.

as much harm to the Enemy as one of Double her force."
He proposed to cruise alone, and asked that Franklin
release to him eight Irish-born prisoners he had brought
into Dunkirk in September. These men preferred service
in the *Fearnot* to rotting in a French jail.

With his belief in Ryan's ability and his desire for more
prisoners, Franklin was most willing to loose a third privateer against British commerce. He sent the commission to
Francis Coffyn and notified Torris to call there for it with
the executed bond. He heartily wished the merchant and
his captain "all the success you desire and deserve." In
writing to Ryan, the Doctor agreed to the shipping of the
eight Irish prisoners although it meant that the British
subjects now left for exchange at Dunkirk had almost
reached the vanishing point.

"I received yours of the 29th. past, am glad to hear that
your Health is re-established, and that you have got a
Vessel that you desire, to which I make no doubt you will
do honour by your Bravery and good Conduct," Franklin's
letter began. "No regard being paid in England to the
written Paroles of discharged Prisoners taken in your
former Voyages nor a man returned in Exchange for them
& 220 more taken by other American Privateers you are
henceforth to secure all your Prisoners as well as you can,
and bring them all into france. I wish you a prosperous
Cruise and safe return with much Profit and Honour."

Prize papers covering four of the vessels sent in during
the first half of the joint cruise began to arrive at Passy for
Franklin's judgment. Those for the fifth, the brig *Betsey*,
examined by the Brest officers, were misdirected to the
High Admiral of France and apparently became lost in his
files. Prompt and painstaking attention was given each
lengthy procès-verbal. No matter how distasteful the task,
nor how great the eye strain in perusing the cramped
French handwriting, the Doctor never again would permit

himself to be charged with delaying condemnation proceedings. He found the papers in order and pronounced all
four to be good prizes.

Not so, however, the papers for two of the three prizes
sent in during the second half of the cruise. Upon the brig
*Philip* he pronounced rapid judgment as a legitimate
capture. About the brig *Friendship* and schooner *Peter* he
had grave doubts. The procès-verbal for each was incomplete. Neither contained an examination of former
crew members; nor was either accompanied by any ship's
papers showing registry, ownership, destination, or cargo.
Franklin spoke his mind to the Admiralty officer who had
forwarded them from Morlaix. He could not give judgment in the absence of such essential documents, lest one
or the other turn out to be a neutral or friendly vessel.

"If we are to condemn Vessels on the bare Declaration
of the Captors without farther Proof," he pointed out,
"Piracies might be by that means encouraged."

The cartel had arrived, meanwhile, with one hundred
American prisoners. Upon this welcome news Franklin
applied to M. de Sartine for an equal number of Britishers
"to be rendered at Morlaix for the exchange." He was
advised that orders would be issued at once to march them
from the prison at Saumur, some two hundred miles southeast of the port of embarkation. David Hartley had written
that until he heard to the contrary, he would assume "that
any Cartel ship of ours will find 100 prisoners at Morlaix."
That seemed a safe premise Franklin thought. In view of
the credit of five hundred British prisoners due him from
the French, he would have no trouble in meeting the re-
quirement.

Hartley's letter had confirmed the refusal of the British
Admiralty to recognize paroles given at sea. The explanation was that the proposition gave greater advantage to
an American captor because, by discharging prisoners, he

could cruise longer and take more prizes than could a British captor who had no such privilege. It was a competitive theory which Hartley said shocked him to recite, and made him "grieve for the Consequences as augmenting the miseries of mankind in war." To that the Doctor could add a fervent "Amen." The decision blasted all hope of reviving the issue, so he was well pleased he had anticipated it with orders to liberate no more Britishers at sea. And he was happy, as he wrote M. de Sartine, that "the Black Prince, the Black Princess and the Fearnot American Privateers are I suppose now on a new Cruise, and will I hope bring in more English prisoners."

Alas for suppositions! The month of April with its springtime blossoms came to Passy and with it came news that the *Fearnot,* delayed in outfitting, had not sailed from Dunkirk until the last week in March; that the *Black Princess,* considered unseaworthy, probably would do more privateering, and that the *Black Prince,* deprived of all French seamen by an arbitrary ruling of the commissary at Morlaix, was too shorthanded to proceed on a cruise. All this was discouraging enough, but more disquieting still was the news delivered by William Hodgson from London.

The cartel ship had returned from Morlaix without a single British prisoner in exchange!

Franklin scarcely could believe the words that leaped out at him from the letter: "I heard this from Plym° & have since been desired to go to the Sick & Hurt Office who confirm'd the Acc't, they appear to be very much disgusted at the proceedings & say it is a breach of Faith." All the cartel had brought back was a certificate from the French commissary acknowledging receipt of one hundred Americans, but stating that he had no English prisoners on hand to return. "I hope Sir you will furnish me with such an explanation of this affair as shall be satisfactory & expedite future exchanges," Hodgson concluded, "at present untill y^e affair is cleared up all further progress in this business must be put a Stop to."

The startled and dismayed Franklin had no immediate explanation to offer. For once, his inventive mind could evoke no ready response. A week elapsed before he learned that the British prisoners never had been sent from Saumur. M. de Sartine offered no explanations, but was most apologetic. He promised Franklin, verbally however, that two hundred would be dispatched immediately by cartel to England to pay for the one hundred Americans received at Morlaix and for a fresh exchange of a similarly sized group. He also assured the Doctor, still verbally, that he would take the earliest opportunity to send the remainder to equal the number delivered in Holland, "having no scruples of doing this by advance."

To all these pledges, the Minister of Marine promised a confirmatory letter, and Franklin advised Hodgson on April 11 that he would forward this letter, when received, to "clear me from any charge of bad faith." But, as he well realized, somebody's stupid blunder bid fair to nullify all his carefully laid plans to redeem his countrymen from captivity.[4]

---

[4] The fiasco of the empty cartel led Franklin into a long letter to M. de Vergennes based largely upon M. de Sartine's failure to live up to his verbal agreement about prisoners. It is in Letter Books, 1780, and is printed in Smyth (ed.), *Writings of Benjamin Franklin*, VIII, 66–68.

CHAPTER XII

# Three Cruises
# and a Shipwreck

LUKE RYAN in the *Fearnot* with a crew of
ninety-six men—forty-five Americans and Irish, and the
balance French, Spanish, Italian, and Portuguese—had
cleared Dunkirk on March 24. The British intelligence
service had advance news of their departure, but had mistaken the objective. In Dublin, advice reached the Lord
Lieutenant of Ireland "that Luke Ryan, the former captain of the Black Prince privateer, was to sail from Dunkirk
as Captain of another privateer, mounting 18 six and nine
pounders, to cruise, as it is supposed, on the coast of this
kingdom." Instead, the venturesome Ryan essayed the far
more dangerous feat of sailing northward into the German
Ocean, and completely encircling England and Scotland.
His audacity and courage was attested to by a Continental
officer, who went with him on a subsequent cruise.

"I have sailed with many brave men, Com. John Paul
Jones &c.," he wrote, "yet none of them equal to this Capt.
Luke Ryon [*sic*] for skill and bravery." [1]

[1] This praise of Luke Ryan was sung by John Trevett, of Rhode Island,
whose journal was partially printed in the *Rhode Island Historical Maga-
zine* (Newport, 1885–87). Its continuation, including the quotation
given, appeared weekly in the [Newport] *Rhode Island Republican,* from
May 8 to June 12, 1839.

The *Fearnot's* armament was not as heavy as John Torris had told Franklin it would be, or as the Lord Lieutenant reported. She carried eighteen guns all right, but only fourteen of them were 6-pounders, and none were of heavier metal. She also carried twelve swivels instead of the promised twenty. Even so, she was well armed, and as Ryan soon discovered, a good sailer.

Luck at first, however, was not good. Until the end of March she encountered neither British warship nor merchantman. Not until April 2, when she had climbed the latitudes to abreast of the Orkney Islands, was she rewarded with a prize. On that day, thirteen leagues southeast of Fair Island, lying midway between the most northern of the Orkneys and the southern tip of Shetland, she took the brig *Noble Anne* of Newcastle, coming from the Greenland fisheries and bound for the river Tyne. Ryan removed master and crew, placed a prizemaster and a few hands on board and sent her almost due eastward for the neutral port of Bergen, in the Norwegian province of Denmark.

During the ensuing six days, the *Fearnot* rounded the Orkneys, slipped down the North and Little Minch channels through the Hebrides, and emerged out of Barra passage into the Atlantic. Late on the afternoon of April 8, some twenty leagues north of Ireland, she encountered the ship *Friends,* Captain Sinclair, a heavily armed letter of marque, bound from the Clyde for Quebec with bale goods. The *Friends* showed fight. Ryan closed in, pounding her with well-aimed broadsides for twenty-five minutes, when she struck. Her return fire had been ineffective, inflicting no damage upon the privateer. Captain Sinclair and most of his crew were transferred to the *Fearnot*. Mate, cabin boy, and two passengers were left in the ship, on board of which Ryan placed a prize crew of twenty-one Frenchmen. The *Friends* had received two shots at the water's edge. A carpenter's crew patched the holes, while the French hands manned the pumps. She went off finally for France in a heavy gale and dark weather, and with six feet of water in her hold. She was never heard of again.

Luke cruised northward toward Barra Head and on April 11 made his third prize, the ship *Jean,* Captain Brown, from Liverpool for Lubeck on the Baltic, with a cargo of salt. According to a British account, "Ryan offered to ransom the Jeane, but at a higher rate than Capt. Brown would give, therefore put her up for sale and was purchased by Capt. Sinclair." The price was 5,000 guineas. Luke took the opportunity to divest himself of fifty-one prisoners. This disregard of Franklin's orders, "to secure all your Prisoners as well as you can and bring them all in to France," he justified by reason of distance from home, insufficient provisions, and weakness of his crew through manning two prizes. He did take sea paroles from his prisoners for whatever they might be worth. The *Jean* was released on April 13, off the Island of Mull.

The *Fearnot* then ran northward through the Gulf of Hebrides toward Canna Island, in search of a vessel reported to have passed that way. The unsuspecting quarry had put into Canna for refreshments, and was overtaken on April 14. She was the ship *Fortitude,* bound from Workington on the Solway Firth for Hull on the English east coast with a cargo of iron ore. He ransomed her and paroled her crew. On board the *Fearnot* now were two hostages, one each for the *Jean* and *Fortitude,* but no other prisoners. Around the end of April, with provisions running lower, Ryan headed homeward. Whether he went through the North Passage and the Irish Sea or ran down the west coast of Ireland is not in the record. That he reached Dunkirk safely is evident by Torris' report to Franklin, that "Cap$^t$. Ryan had greatly distinguished himself in the Fearnot, who is now here under repairs to

Continue Shortly his Cruise." To this the Doctor replied with congratulations upon his success.[2]

Patrick Dowlin's troubles with his French seamen were due, according to Torris, to "The Self Conceited & Weak Commissary of Morlaix." That individual, again to quote the Dunkirk merchant, was "really watchful of all opportunity to molest all americans & Specially the Captains & officers of our Privateers." The results were disastrous for the *Black Prince*. Although the mutinous Frenchmen still had a month more of service under their contracts, they refused to cruise longer, and appealed to the commissary. He came on board and, despite the captain's protests, discharged all of them.

With a crew reduced to fifty-three officers and men, Dowlin departed from Morlaix and skirted the coast to Roscoff. At Mr. Clancey's he found the letter Franklin had written to him in February. He was sorry he had not received it sooner, he informed the Doctor on April 3, as he might have made different disposition of the prisoners he had paroled in the ransomed packets. What most disturbed him, however, was the interference of the commissary at Morlaix, whose action he considered "Contrary to the Interests of the United States." Loss of the French hands put an end to further cruising and forced him to return to Dunkirk "with the few Country Men I have." He was cleaning the cutter and securing provisions, after which he hoped "to Annoy the Enemy in our Passage."

The *Black Prince* sailed from Roscoff on April 6. Next day, northwestward of the Channel Islands, Dowlin

[2] The cruise of the *Fearnot* was given far more attention in the English newspapers than in Franklin's correspondence. One of the best accounts of the successful operations south of the Hebrides was contained in a letter from Glasgow, printed in the London *Chronicle*, April 22–25, 1780. A letter from Kirkwall, published in *ibid.*, May 13–16, 1780, adds much additional information.

boarded the Dutch ship *Flora,* Henry Rodenberg, master, and owned by a firm of Rotterdam merchants. She was bound for Dublin. Before dismissing her as a neutral, he questioned the master and examined her papers. Rodenberg admitted that his cargo of grain, drugs and spice had been shipped on order of Dublin merchants. The bills of lading confirmed this. The vessel might well be Dutch-owned, Dowlin thought, but her contents looked like enemy property. He removed the master and her four hands, further reduced his own small complement by a prize crew, and ordered the *Flora* for Cherbourg.

The *Black Prince* continued up channel. In another twenty-four hours she had an engagement with an armed cutter, but when two British frigates appeared, she broke it off abruptly and made for the shelter of the French shore. The following morning she came up with a brig which looked a likely prize. Before the quarry could be boarded, a frigate stretched out from the land and stood toward them. Dowlin fled incontinently. By then the *Black Prince* was well along on her homeward way, running northward off the coast of Picardy. The frigate, flying English colors, kept upon her heels through the ensuing afternoon and night (despite shoals and shallows).

By morning there was little wind, but pursuit continued. Around noon Dowlin fired three guns to leeward and hoisted French colors, a recognition signal. It was ignored. An hour later he repeated the performance, again with no response. Desperate now, the Irish captain turned his bow shoreward, ran in close under the land, once more flew the French flag, and fired signals of distress to attract assistance from several small forts. He was off the rugged coast between Berck and Estaples, towns some ten leagues south of Boulogne.

Several thousand excited spectators lined the headlands as cutter and frigate approached. By late afternoon, the pursuer was within pistol shot of the privateer. She was also within long range of the guns of the fort at Berck, which opened upon her. The climax came abruptly. Even as the reverberations of the first discharge rolled seaward, the *Black Prince* piled upon the rocks. The frigate, already in less than three fathoms of water, lowered her English colors, hoisted the fleur de lis, and sheered off. Dowlin and all hands, including the captive Captain Rodenberg and his four Dutch sailors, reached shore in safety. Most of the cutter's equipment was gotten out in the subsequent twenty-four hours, but the little privateer was a shattered wreck.

The master of the *Flora* was hauled before a Berck magistrate where he made deposition "that his cargo was for the account of the merchants of Dublin." Shortly after that John Torris arrived posthaste, and "had the mortification to See the reck of our poor privateer, which deserved a better fate." He, Dowlin and his crew, and Rodenberg and his seamen then proceeded southward across the mouth of the Somme to St. Valery, seeking the necessary Admiralty officers for preparation of a procès-verbal. M. Lefebvre, the merchant's correspondent in St. Valery, took the Dutchmen in charge while the others then set off for Dunkirk, Torris vowing that "I wou'd Sooner Sell my Last Shirt than not procure Soon a Large Cutter for the Intrepid & Clever Capt[n] Dowlin."

The party reached its destination on the night of April 14, and learned that the vessel which had driven the *Black Prince* ashore had not been English, but the French frigate *Calonne!* She had been commanded, according to Torris, "by the Ignorant Capt[n] Guilman," who had run into Dunkirk and made a report of the affair "fit to Justiffy him Self." Off to Franklin next day went an urgent plea that complaints be lodged with the Minister of Marine against the commissary at Morlaix and the captain of the frigate,

"Because The Conduct of both is no Way Tollerable, re-
quires punishment & damages." [3]

While the *Black Prince* was coming to grief, Edward
Macatter had gathered the remnants of his crew together
in Morlaix and marched them to Cherbourg. Like Dowlin,
he had been deprived of all French seamen, but he was
still fortunate in holding on to Charles Collins and some
of the nineteen Americans who had escaped from Pembroke Castle. "The Old & unfit princess" had been laid up
at Morlaix, and Torris had promised a larger cutter with
the same name at Cherbourg. Thus, commission and bond
need not be changed. The new *Black Princess* was all that
could be desired. She carried eighteen 6-pounders, two
stern-chase 9-pounders, and thirty swivels—a redoubtable
armament indeed.

To man her was the real problem. Cherbourg was not
a smuggling center like Dunkirk. There were few idle
hands about. Torris' agent, M. de Chautereyne, united
with Macatter in appealing to the commissaries at Havre
and Cherbourg "as much for obtaining Irish sailors as well
as foreigners who are in various prisons or come in prizes."
M. de Chautereyne suggested to Franklin that a word
of recommendation from him to these commissaries would
prove helpful.

The *Flora* sailed into Cherbourg on April 9, and was
duly entered as a prize. Word was sent to Torris of her
arrival, while the Admiralty registrar set a guard upon her
and sealed her hatches. The Dunkirk merchant, mean-

[3] John Torris worked himself up into a furious state over "the Ignorant
Capt[n]. Guilman, who made a report here on the Subject, fit to Justiffy him
Self, but the guard of the Fort that fired on his frigate, & thousands people
on the shore who saw every thing of this stupid & Villanous Chace will
Certify . . . that She Shewed her Self Clear to every-body to be an English
Frigate." Torris' letter is in Franklin Papers, APS, where will be found
other letters regarding the loss of the *Black Prince* and problems in con-
demning the cargo of the ship *Flora*.

while, had had disturbing news from St. Valery. A Dutch interpreter had approached Captain Rodenberg and induced him to make out a new report. Its contents had been withheld from M. Lefebvre, but, it was understood, it repudiated his Berck declaration. The Dutch captain also had refused to accept "conduct Money" so he and his crew could rejoin their ship. His excuse was reluctance to leave before receiving orders from Rotterdam. M. Lefebvre's suspicions that the interpreter had so advised were confirmed when the latter sent Rodenberg off to Cherbourg, and supplied travel funds.

This alarming situation put John Torris on the move; first, to St. Valery where he had access to the new report, and then to Cherbourg. Rodenberg was again examined and repudiated his St. Valery declaration, reaffirming the one made at Berck. The procès-verbal was completed and forwarded to the Council of Prizes. To leave no loophole, Torris engaged a celebrated attorney named Groute, to render an opinion upon the legality of condemning the cargo. Not content with that, the merchant rushed off to Paris, and was assured the procès-verbal had cleared the Council of Prizes and had been sent to Franklin. Back again in Dunkirk by May 13, he advised the Doctor that the varied testimonies of "the perjured Capt$^n$. Rodenberg," and "the fraudulent forms of the Bills of Lading" must clearly prove that the cargo had been enemy property.

At Cherbourg, meanwhile, manning the *Black Princess* had proceeded slowly. The commissaries there and at Havre had not been co-operative, nor had Franklin sent any recommendations to them. Her complement was fixed at ninety men, but by mid-May she could muster but seventy-five. The captain made up his mind to proceed to sea shorthanded. By a coincidence too strange to be credited, it happened that as Macatter was getting under way on the night of departure, fifteen French sailors came alongside in a small boat, and "offer'd them Selves for the Time of the Cruise." How they knew the *Black Princess* was going out that night and that she needed exactly fifteen more seamen were questions not asked by the captain "who took 'em on thinking no harm in doing so."

The cutter slipped forth by dawn, stretching westward toward Start Point on the English shore. On May 25, off Bolt Head, where the coast rounds into Bigbury Bay, she spied and chased a brig. Pursuit was brief, the *Black Princess* rapidly overhauling her quarry. Macatter ordered a gun to bring her to. At the first shot the brig's crew piled into a boat and pulled for the nearby strand. When the privateer drew abreast, only the master remained on board. She had a cargo of barley and was well worth sending in. Another sail was discerned to the westward and Macatter was anxious to be off. He sent one of his Americans as prizemaster and four French seamen as crew. No one on board the *Black Princess* ascertained the brig's name, port of departure, or destination. Her master, who could have supplied all this, had been left in her. As two days later she was retaken, Macatter never learned anything more about his first capture in his new command.[4]

For the next few days the *Black Princess* cruised off Falmouth and Lizard Point with disappointing results. Then the picture changed. At daybreak on May 29, the ship *George,* from London for Dublin, was boarded and ransomed, her master being taken off as hostage. In rapid succession, they intercepted the sloop *Saville,* from Plymouth for Liverpool; the brigantine *Fortune's Favour,* a coaster from Guernsey; and the sloop *Triton,* from Tingmouth to Liverpool, taking a ransomer from each. Toward

---

4 The only identification of this prize is contained in a list of Mill Prison captives, and reads: "Black Princess (a French Vessel) Prize, taken May 27, 1780, committed July 17, 1780, Edward Huling, Salem." [Philadelphia] *Pennsylvania Packet or General Advertiser,* May 23, 1782.

noon they captured the brig *Live Oak,* from Lymington near Portsmouth, for Bristol. They now had six hostages for five ransoms, totaling £3,700. Macatter had extracted paroles from all members of the released crews, but had placed no prisoners in the *Black Princess.* He was reserving the hold for future captives, rather than encumber himself so early in the cruise.

Three armed vessels spoiled his plans. His Majesty's schooner *Racehorse* and two British privateers, the cutter *Unicorn* and brig *Alligator,* had sailed from Falmouth that morning in quest of the marauder who had been cruising so audaciously off the coast. They came in sight as Macatter was dismissing the *Live Oak.* He spread all the canvas the *Black Princess* could bear and ran southward, the trio stringing out in pursuit, the cutter *Unicorn* in the van. For seven hours he fled. Fleet as the *Black Princess* was, the foremost pursuer was just a little bit fleeter, and gradually cut down the distance between them. She finally drew abreast and opened fire.

This was the first battle-testing of Macatter's hands. They responded nobly. An occasional futile 9-pound shot from their stern-chases had been fired, and now they manned the 6-pounders like veterans, which, in the case of the Americans on board, they were. For a half hour the two cutters exchanged broadsides. The enemy fired high, the shot playing havoc with the *Black Princess'* sails and rigging. Macatter's guns were better served, concentrating upon their opponent's deck. One fortunate shot dismasted the *Unicorn.* As her spars and sails came down in a tangled mass, the *Black Princess* shot ahead out of range. Macatter dared not pause to rake and subdue his enemy for the schooner and brig were coming up too fast. So he fled anew until the British vessels abandoned the chase.

The *Black Princess* had not a man killed or wounded. Macatter did make an unpleasant discovery, however: his adversary, in direct defiance of the laws of nations, had been firing glass bottles. Fragments were found sticking in the mast and yards, and more than a bushel of glass splinters was swept up on deck. The pursuit had carried them well along toward the coast of France, and the captain judged it better to make for Morlaix for repairs rather than attempt them at sea. They rounded the Isle of Bas, and entered the roadstead on the first day of June.

Macatter communicated with John Diot and reported his arrival to the Admiralty. Naïvely or thoughtlessly, in supplying the French authorities with the required crew list, he included the names of his French hands. These fifteen were not merchant seamen, but sailors of the Royal navy, and their surreptitious departure from Cherbourg in the *Black Princess* already had been communicated to the Admiralty in all ports the privateer might enter. That same commissary Torris had complained so bitterly about in April saw his opportunity and descended upon Macatter and Diot the very day of arrival. He had orders, he announced, not to let the privateer go out again until instructions came from Versailles. He demanded that all fifteen Frenchmen be delivered to him on the morrow. The captain pointed out that this was impossible as four of them were still out in a prize. To complicate matters still further, three of the eleven remaining on board deserted in the night. The infuriated commissary threatened next morning to clap Macatter into Morlaix jail.

Much disturbed, Diot appealed to Franklin. The captain was innocent of intended wrongdoing. He was ignorant, as any foreigner would be, of French laws and customs, and if he had been in error, "he knew no better and Methinks it Ought to be taken into Consideration." Diot was upset, too, about the use of glass bottles by the *Black Princess'* opponent. He believed the Doctor should represent the matter to the English ministry, "For any man that is wounded So, is unrecoverable." Reprisals might ensue also, for, knowing the tempers of his Irishmen, he was sure they "wou'd Sink any English privateer that wou'd henceforth Use So illegal a practise." The action of the Morlaix commissary, Diot attributed "to his Spiteful and Rough ungentleman like Temper and Endeed, it's Shocking the way that Americans are used by him."

The commissary, despite all pleas, was adamant. While Macatter escaped prison bars, the French seamen were removed. The privateer lay impotent in the roadstead, under the guns of the French fort, in the face of intelligence that a fleet of three hundred British merchantmen, under a light convoy, had sailed from Tor Bay.[5]

5 John Diot in two letters in Franklin Papers, APS, supplies detailed accounts of Macatter's cruise in the *Black Princess* and his troubles with the commissary of the port. The London *Courant*, June 13, 1780, gives the British version of the engagement between the *Black Princess* and the privateer *Unicorn*.

## CHAPTER XIII

# Dr. Franklin's Troubles Multiply

OF ALL THE PRIZE papers sent him since his privateers first took to the sea, Benjamin Franklin liked least the procès-verbal relating to the Dutch ship *Flora*. Examination by the Admiralty judges at Cherbourg had disclosed that the ship definitely was owned by a Rotterdam firm, but that her cargo, while not contraband, seemed to be the property of merchants in Dublin. The six-page brief prepared by M. Groute, the counsellor-at-law engaged by John Torris, presented impressive arguments justifying "confiscation of all enemy cargoes," and cited more authorities than the Doctor had ever heard of.[1]

It was not the legality, but the wisdom of condemning the cargo that gave Franklin pause. For more than a hundred years the doctrine of Consolato del Mare had prevailed—that enemy property, contraband or not, was subject to capture on board neutral vessels. Based upon that doctrine, it was clear to him that the *Flora* should be freed, and the goods she carried condemned to the captors.

[1] M. Groute, "Councellor at law," wrote his observations in French on May 3, 1780, and at very great length. The document is in the Franklin Papers, Historical Society of Pennsylvania, along with a covering letter of M. de Chautereyne.

But Catharine II of Russia had just proposed an armed neutrality wherein the goods of the belligerent nations, except contraband, should be free on board neutral vessels. Most of the European countries whose good will Franklin coveted were likely to join with Russia. So he consulted John Adams and Francis Dana, two gentlemen an optimistic Continental Congress had just sent to Europe to negotiate a peace treaty with Great Britain. Their advice was to follow the established rule—release the ship, condemn the cargo, and pay her owners the full freight. Franklin took their counsel and hoped it would prove satisfactory.

"But it is a critical time with respect to such cases," he wrote Congress, "for whatever may formerly have been the law of nations, all the neutral powers at the instance of Russia, seem at present disposed to change it, and so enforce the rule that *free ships make free goods,* except in the case of contraband." [2]

His decision went to the judges of the Admiralty at Cherbourg on May 16. The *Flora* was not a good prize, but, said he: "The Cargo is really the property of the Subjects of the King of England, tho attempted to be masq'd as neutral." He went on to request that the cargo be landed, the ship be restored to Captain Rodenberg, the captors be obliged to pay him full freight according to his bills of lading, and make good all damages he might have sustained by plunder. Then he took a further precaution. As the cargo was perishable, it should be sold, and the proceeds held by the Admiralty until all probabilities of litigation were at an end.

A copy of this judgment he enclosed to Torris on May 27, in a rather scathing letter relating not to the *Flora,* but

[2] The armed neutrality of 1780 is discussed at considerable length in Samuel Flagg Bemis, *The Diplomacy of the American Revolution* (New York, 1935), 151–161,

to the brig *Friendship* and schooner *Peter*, which vessels he had refused previously to condemn without ship's papers or prisoners to be examined. There had been sufficient time to send the papers to Passy, Franklin said, and he had begun to suspect that they were withheld because they would show both vessels were neutrals. The Dunkirk merchant had suggested that the paroles signed at sea by the crews of the *Friendship* and *Peter* be consulted. These would prove, Torris had remarked, that they "were manned entirely with British Subjects, therefore were English Bottoms, & of Course good Prises." Franklin took sharp exception to this contention. "You mention as a Proof an agreement sent to me, as sign'd by the Prisoners when discharged acknowledging themselves English, &c.," he wrote. "I received that Paper but I observe that the names were all sign'd in one hand Writing which is another suspicious Circumstance."

Several days later, he remembered that he had intended to issue absolute orders against bringing in any more Dutch vessels unless their cargoes clearly were contraband. He remedied his omission on May 30, with a second letter to Torris, in which he outlined the principle being laid down by the neutral powers, and continued:

> This rule is in itself so reasonable, and of a nature so beneficial to man, that I cannot but wish it may become general, and I make no doubt but that the Congress will agree to it in as full an extent as france and Spain. In the mean time, and until I have received their Orders on the Subject, it is my Intention to condemn no more English goods found in Dutch vessels unless contraband; of which I thought it right to give you this previous Notice, that you may avoid the Trouble and Expense likely to arise from such Captures, and the Detention of them for a decision.

While he had condemned the *Flora*'s cargo largely because "the English have in the West Indies confiscated several of our cargoes found in Dutch ships," Franklin's humanitarian instincts prompted a wish that the new doctrine would go much further; further, in fact, than to this day has been accepted by warring mankind. He proposed in a letter to one of his numerous correspondents, that "the husbandmen on their lands, fishermen in their barks and traders in unarmed vessels shall be permitted to prosecute their several innocent and useful employments without interruption or molestation."

The affairs of the *Flora* were not ended for Franklin, with the dispatch of his judgment to Cherbourg. Her owners had complained to the States General of Holland, who, in turn, had instructed their Ambassador at Versailles to demand restoration of ship and cargo. The Ambassador's remonstrance to M. de Sartine was forwarded in due course to M. de Vergennes, Minister for Foreign Affairs. In communicating it, the Minister of Marine had commented upon the "inconvenience resulting from American privateers fitted out as the Black Prince is, by Frenchmen, and yet not subject to the same forms and laws with our privateers." Vergennes forwarded the protest and M. de Sartine's letter to Passy on June 17, requesting an explanation.

Franklin was disturbed at and provoked by M. de Sartine's uncalled-for comment. It had been he who had evolved the regulations of 1778—under which prizes brought in by American privateers were to be handled in France. Likewise, Sartine had been familiar with every step the Doctor had taken in commissioning the *Black Prince, Black Princess,* and *Fearnot.* Now, as soon as a complaint was received, the Minister of Marine was seeking to shift responsibility elsewhere. So Franklin gave his explanation with no equivocation. He enclosed a copy of his judgment on the *Flora,* so Vergennes could see "that I have already given orders for the release of the vessel, with payment of damages, before the ambassador's complaint was made." He had condemned the cargo for three sound reasons: first, because "the law has been settled in America that enemies' property found in neutral ships might be taken out of the same"; second, because the English had been doing just that to American goods shipped in Dutch bottoms; and, third, because Holland had taken no notice of a long-proffered treaty "in which there was an article that free ships should make free goods."

Then he paid his respects to M. de Sartine's comment. The commissions he had granted specified that prizes carried into a foreign state should be submitted to the judgment of the admiralty courts. Several of the first prizes brought in were so judged, and, said the Doctor with some emphasis, "it was not upon any request of mine that such causes were afterwards referred to me, nor am I desirous of continuing to exercise that jurisdiction. If, therefore, the judgment I have given in the case of the Flora is not approved, and the Council of Prizes will take the trouble of ex-examining and trying that cause and those of all other prizes to be brought in hereafter by American cruisers, it will be very agreeable to me . . . and I think it will also be agreeable to Congress."

He had no desire, he continued, to encourage the King's subjects to fit out privateers in France with American commissions. In fact, he had refused many such applications and had advised them to apply for French commissions. The case of the *Black Prince* was, as he expressed it, "peculiar." He then proceeded to enlighten Vergennes upon the smuggling history of the little cutter, and how her crew had cut her out of Poolbeg.

"It was represented to me," he resumed, "that the people, being English and Irish, were afraid to continue their smuggling business, lest if they should be again taken they might be punished as British subjects for their crime at Dublin, and that they were willing to go a privateering against the English; but speaking no other language, they imagined they might, if taken, better pass as Americans if they had an American commission, than as Frenchmen, if under a French commission."

For that reason he had granted the commission, feeling that "a crew that knew so well all parts of the enemy's coasts, might greatly molest their coasting trade." Her success had been such that her owners had added the *Black Princess,* also with an American commission, "and between them they have taken and sent in, or ransomed, or destroyed, an amazing number of vessels; I think near eighty." Franklin studiously avoided any reference to the *Fearnot,* a point to be borne in mind. He concluded by informing Vergennes that he would grant no more commissions, except to American-owned vessels, and, if the Minister desired, he would recall those issued to the *Black Prince* and the *Black Princess.* As the former lay a hopeless wreck off Berck, his amiable gesture has to be discounted fifty per cent.[3]

Franklin's seeming willingness to abandon his privateering ventures was in no sense a loss of interest in the fate of the American prisoners in England. Their liberation was still uppermost in his mind, but there seemed almost a conspiracy on foot to thwart his every effort. The case of the empty cartel at Morlaix in April was an example of the way he had been frustrated. It demonstrated, as well, the shifty tactics of M. de Sartine even as had the matter of the *Flora.* The promises from the Minister of Marine to supply the deficit and even to add a hundred more British

---

[3] Franklin's letter of June 18, 1780 was about the longest he ever wrote to M. de Vergennes. It is printed in Wharton (ed.), *Revolutionary Diplomatic Correspondence,* III, 801–803. As Vergennes' letter that provoked it and much that had gone before regarding the *Flora* is omitted in Wharton, Franklin's letter scarcely can be appreciated by itself.

prisoners to compensate for not sending the first hundred to the cartel ship had been oral ones. Franklin had accepted them in good faith, understanding there would be confirmation by letter. But there never was. Nor were M. de Sartine's repeated pledges realized—to furnish a total of five hundred prisoners (the equivalent of those exchanged for Frenchmen in Holland) and thus effect the release of all Americans in captivity in Great Britain. Pressing for fulfillment, the Doctor learned, to his utter disgust, that the Minister of Marine now disavowed any such authority, and advised that "the king's order is necessary to be first obtained."

That was disheartening enough, but on top of that, Franklin had more disquieting news from William Hodgson in London. Hodgson had discovered at the Board of Sick and Hurt "a very great Reluctance to accept French captured Prisoners in lieu of American captured ones." He had pointed out to the Board that the idea had originated with it in exchanging John Paul Jones's prisoners in Holland for Frenchmen, and it certainly could not, with propriety, be now disclaimed. But as the merchant reminded Franklin, "You know, much better than I that it avails little to urge any Arguments if there is not a private Disposition to hearken to them."

The Doctor went through the gesture of appealing to Vergennes to secure the King's permission to furnish the five hundred prisoners. He could, however, see its futility now that Great Britain would not accept them in exchange for Americans. Just as futile, apparently, were his hopes that his privateers would bring in sufficient prisoners to fill an occasional cartel. Both the *Black Princess* and *Fearnot* had returned from successful cruises with numerous paroles taken at sea, but not a Britisher confined below deck; yet each captain had received his instructions to bring them in and not release them. It was almost too much! He lashed at Torris on June 26, for this disobedience of orders:

> When a Commission was ask'd for the Princess, I was told that Cruizing together there would be more convenience to stow and bring in Prisoners, but the contrary has happen'd fewer being brought in than before. The Prisoners to exchange for Americans are all the Advantage I have for my trouble in reading and examining the Admiralty Papers, and for the vast Expence to Postage these Pacquets of Papers, and the Correspondence relating to the Captures occasion me. Not one American Prisoner has ever been return'd me from England in consequence of the Paroles given by the English Prisoners discharged at Sea. So that if that Practice is continued I must decline farther Concern in the affair and withdraw the Commissions.

Goaded, meanwhile, by Franklin's insinuations that the *Friendship* and *Peter* probably were neutral vessels, Patrick Dowlin had searched the papers he had saved from the wreck of the *Black Prince,* and had found "2 Letters, a Bill of Lading, a Draught & 2 accounts, fully proving what the Friendship and her Cargoe are." These were forwarded to Passy along with explanations that the master of each vessel had signed the paroles for all crew members, filling in their names. Torris also secured through a London correspondent, an affidavit from Thomas Byrne, master of the *Peter,* clearly establishing her British ownership. In the face of all this evidence, Franklin condemned the brig and schooner, but refused to act upon the brig *Betsey,* taken in December. No evidence had been sent to him that she was English property, and he remarked with thinly veiled sarcasm, that "whatever good Opinion I may have of the Uprightness of your Captains it is not regular that I should condemn without Proof."

Torris had expressed dissatisfaction with Franklin's decision upon the *Flora,* particularly the impounding of the receipts from the sale of her cargo. The merchant had no intention of appealing to Congress, he hastened to explain, but he felt the cost of the freight and the damages to the master's property should be paid out of the funds held by the Admiralty, and not out of the pockets of the captors from whom the proceeds had been withheld. He also complained that Franklin had set no time limit for freighters to make their claims or file appeals to Congress, and the cause, consequently, might go on indefinitely.

Awaiting the French Court's decision upon the *Flora,* Franklin was not disposed to give Torris' pleas much consideration. He contented himself by advising that he had given a copy of his decision to the agent for the owner of the Dutch ship, who, perhaps, might also have some objections.[4] If so, he would find it more convenient to consider the whole together. And that, as it later turned out, was all the satisfaction John Torris was to receive.

[4] "We have received the letter you have done us the honor of writing on May 28 with the copy of the judgment for the ship Flora and its cargo," Vandenyver Bros. & Co., the agents, had written to Franklin on June 22, 1780. "We had hoped that it would be more favorable to the owners of the last, but we have sent it immediately to Cherbourg in order to have it put into execution." This letter is in Franklin Papers, APS; Franklin to Torris, in Letter Books, 1780.

CHAPTER XIV

# *Reign of the* Black Princess

D ETENTION OF THE *Black Princess* at Morlaix had continued until the end of June. By the time the antagonistic commissary reluctantly released her upon orders from Versailles, she was provisioned and manned with one hundred and twenty stout men. All French hands were gone, so were most of the Americans, five only remaining, along with six foreigners—Dutchmen and Portuguese. Irish and English smugglers comprised the balance of the crew, "pirates of the worst sort," as one of their subsequent victims would call them, "with nothing but certain death to expect in consequence of being taken." Edward Macatter had hoped for a larger complement. He had asked permission to recruit among British prisoners in Dinan Castle, in eastern Brittany, but had been refused. Despite the rebuff, he could pride himself upon the most hard-bitten crew he had ever commanded when the heavily armed cutter cleared the Isle of Bas roadstead on June 29.

The course was northward across the English Channel, around Land's End and along the coast of Cornwall toward Lundy Island in the mouth of Bristol Channel, taking and ransoming numerous prizes as they went. By July 1, Macatter had eight hostages on board, but had retained no prisoners. He had been forced to ransom, as he later explained, because of the smallness of his ship's company. He could ill spare prize crews at the very beginning of his run or encumber himself so soon with captives.

Off Milford Haven next morning they pursued three merchantmen southward bound in St. George's Channel. The rearmost, the brig *Padmore,* was overhauled and boarded. She carried a cargo of considerable value—twenty-four 4-pounders of a new construction from the foundries of Chester and bound for London. Macatter sent William Ripner, one of his valued Americans, to her with a prize crew of three men. The *Padmore*'s master, two women passengers, and four of her six crewmen were removed to the *Black Princess.* The other two Britishers were left in Ripner's charge. He deposited them in Morlaix jail four days later when he brought the prize in after a narrow escape from an English privateer close to the mouth of the harbor.

Chase of the *Padmore* had carried the *Black Princess* well toward the Irish coast. Six leagues off Wexford on the morning of July 4, she came upon the sloop *Betsey* from Liverpool for Youghal with a cargo of salt and coal. The sloop's master was carried on board the cutter and detained until nightfall when he was ransomed and released. From her deck, meanwhile, he had witnessed the capture of three more colliers. Two were from Whitehaven for Waterford; the third, the brig *Three Brothers,* was from Liverpool for Exeter in Devon. Both Waterford-bound vessels were ransomed, some of the *Black Princess'* crew boasting to the masters that, "they knew there was no ship of force on the coast and that they would have the linen ships before they departed." The master of the *Three Brothers,* a stubborn Scot, refused to ransom. Macatter took him and his hands on board the privateers and burned the brig.

Lighted by the flames consuming the *Three Brothers,* the *Black Princess* stood northward. Her course, into and through the Irish Sea, was marked by frequent prizes—a brig off Wicklow Head, two others between Bardsley Island and Holyhead, and a fourth between Holyhead and the Isle of Man. The first three were ransomed for five hundred guineas each. The last victim was the seventy-ton brig *John,* John McIsaacs, master, carrying coal from Campbeltown, on the west bank of the Clyde, for Dublin. One of the privateer's lieutenants boarded the *John,* demanding a ransom of £400. McIsaacs protested. Vessel and cargo, in his estimation, were not worth half that sum. The lieutenant did not argue, but drew his pistol and thrust the muzzle against the master's breast. With his other hand he extended the ransom note.

"Sign this, or else . . . ," he began. McIsaacs signed.

On the night of July 7, the *Black Princess* slipped past Spanish Head and lay to for some hours between the Isle and Calf of Man. Macatter stood out before daybreak next morning, heading for a sail dimly visible to the southward. The quarry was the brig *Nancy and Peggy,* George Cloud, master, bound in for Chester after a long voyage from Riga in the Baltic. Cloud had had a glimpse of the privateer, but it was sunrise before he made her out to be an enemy. Her canvas supplied the telltale mark, French sails being much broader and whiter than English ones. By the time he was sure of her identity, escape was impossible. The *Black Princess* stretched across his bow and hailed: "Heave to! This is a press boat!"

Cloud was not deceived, but he had too few guns to resist. The line of shuttered ports along the cutter's side concealed enough cannon, he knew, to blow him to bits. An officer came blustering over the side, demanded the brig's papers, and announced that the master must return with him to be interrogated.

"You are a rogue," Cloud told him, but realized he had

Brest, Black Prince Jan'y 27th 1780

I left Dunkirk the 21 of last Month upon my Cruize, all hands Well, hard Weather, came to the Lands end of England, and on the 26th of Dec'r and 27th D'o took 3 Valuable Prizes which are Safe Arrived in France besides four Ransoms, I have put into the Prison of Port L'Orient 40 Prisoners which I hope if Mr Torr Kinsey will Approve of as they may be a means of being Exchanged for as many of our Country Men Prisoners in great Britain, our Consort the Princess hath been Prosperous having taken four Prizes, two of whom are Arrived in France and hope the other two are Safe Arrived, but has not heard from them yet I have Gave to Mr Diott a Copy of my Journall and a Copy of the Names of Prisoners, which he is to send to your Excellency, I hope soon to be Ready to set to Sea and Expects and Determines to do as much hurt to the Enemies of United States as possibly can in a day or two I Expect to join Company with the Princess at the Isle of Bass where she now is, and so proceed on our Intended Cruize, If your Excellency Pleases to favour me with an Answer please to Direct to Capt Patt. Dowlin Capt Black Prince, at Mr — Clancey's Merchant in Roscoff, I Rem'n with Respects to all Gentlemen Americans of your Acquaintance Yr P. Patt. Dowlin

PATRICK DOWLIN REPORTS A SUCCESSFUL CRUISE

May it Please Your Excellency

We Humbly beg to Express to Your Excellency Our Gratitude for the Liberty granted us for to serve with Capt. Ryan on Board of his Cutter the Fearnot. We solemnly Promise to Your Excellency to be faithfull in Our services to the Brave Capt. Ryan & To be ever true to Our Oath of Allegiance to the United States of America, which we Now make in the Hands of your Excellency, with our Warmest acknowledgments to have empowered us to do the same, & therewith follow our Inclination,

We Are with Due Respect

May it Please Your Excellency

Dunkerque. the 14th. Feby: 1780.

Your Most Obedient & most Humble Servants

John Stuart
Daniel Sidney
James _____
Walter Beach
Edward _____
George Sidney his mark +
William L. _____ his mark +

His Excellency Doct. Franklin

BRITISH PRISONERS ASK TO SERVE ON THE "FEARNOT"

no alternative. He entered the boat, was taken to the privateer and ushered to the after cabin.

"Welcome to the Black Princess, captain," Macatter greeted him affably. "May I give you a glass of gin and bitters?"

"I've had bitters enough," was Cloud's sour reply.

"Very well, sir, then let's get down to business. Will you ransom your vessel?"

"No!" The master's voice was sharp. Then he paused: "Not unless you will take three hundred pounds."

Macatter smiled. That was somewhat too small an amount for so fine a brig, he commented. He would require not less than six hundred guineas. They haggled a bit until Cloud made what he called his top offer, five hundred guineas.

"Sorry, captain, that's not enough," Macatter said. "If you will not give six hundred guineas, I will have to burn your vessel."

"Use your pleasure, then, for I will pay no more," Cloud answered.

"Come on deck and I'll show you how it's done." Macatter led the way to where the longboat was being loaded with combustibles. Cloud watched it pull away, and followed its course until it had reached the brig's side. Then he capitulated.

"All right, call back your boat," he agreed. "I'll pay six hundred guineas."

The ransom note was signed, while Macatter hailed the brig and ordered his lieutenant to return with a hostage. When Cloud later regained the *Nancy and Peggy,* he found that his chest and case had been broken open, "and every valuable I had was gone, even my very razors and combs. They left me but one shirt, that on my back." As he resumed his interrupted voyage, the *Black Princess* stood toward a distant brig. An hour later, Cloud watched in fascination as flames licked up and around her. The Irish captain very evidently had not been bluffing, the master of the *Nancy and Peggy* concluded.[1]

Identity of the second brig which Macatter burned is not disclosed. Neither is there mention of other prizes to account for twenty-two hostages he had on board including the last one delivered from Cloud's brig. In the hold were sixteen prisoners—part of the crew of the *Padmore,* and of the two burned brigs. The two women from the *Padmore* had been sent off in one of the ransomed vessels. Thirty-eight Britishers had to be guarded day and night. Perhaps at that point Macatter might have headed back, but from Captain Cloud he had learned that two more vessels from the Baltic were a day's sail behind him, coming down through the North Channel after rounding Scotland. Instead of pointing his bow southward, therefore, the course was due north for the mouth of the Clyde.[2]

South of the Mull of Cantyre and abreast of the Irish coast just above the town of Larne, Macatter discovered his quarry—a ship and a brig. It was late afternoon of Sunday, July 9, when he made them out to the eastward. He

---

[1] Captain Cload related his experiences in a letter written after the *Nancy and Peggy* had reached Chester, England. It contained the conversation with Macatter as quoted in the text. The letter was printed in the London *Chronicle,* August 3–5, 1780.

[2] Although the *Black Princess* on the night of July 8 was a good sixty miles north of the packet boat route, Sir John Irvine, commander in chief of His Majesty's forces in Ireland, was sure he had just missed being taken by her in crossing the Irish Sea from Holyhead to Dublin. "I landed here on Saturday night after a most tedious passage and a very narrow escape from the Black Princess," he wrote Lord George Germain on July 11, 1780. "I passed by a vessel about three leagues from the hill of Howth which had been taken and ransomed a few hours before; and I find that within these six days upwards of thirty vessels, chiefly colliers, have been taken by that privateer. The people here complain very much on this subject." The letter is in the Historical Manuscript Commission's *Report on the Manuscripts of Mrs. Stopford-Sackville of Drayton House, Northamptonshire* (London, 1904), I, 270.

veered toward the foremost vessel, the ship. By twilight he was within hail, the brig being several miles astern. His opponent was the *Crow Castle,* Captain Robinson, a letter of marque carrying ten 6-pounders and a crew of twenty-four. When the cutter was spied steering directly for them out of the west with St. George's colors flying, Robinson had suspected an enemy and cleared ship for action. The *Black Princess* ranged up under the ship's starboard quarter, the British flag still apeak.

Someone hailed from the *Crow Castle:* "What ship is that?"

The answer came down the wind: "Strike, or I'll sink you!"

At the same moment the red St. George's cross was jerked to the deck, the thirteen stripes rose to replace it, and a broadside from the *Black Princess'* larboard battery lashed the enemy. Then she veered, crossed her wake and came up on the larboard quarter to deliver a broadside from the starboard 6-pounders. The ship's guns responded, and acrid powder smoke engulfed the combatants. Time and again the *Black Princess* strove to board, but was checked by the well-directed and furious fire from the *Crow Castle,* or balked by the masterful way Captain Robinson maneuvered his vessel to elude the cutter's grappling irons. The *Black Princess'* guns, too, were well served. They aimed high—at the masts—but to no avail. Subsequently Robinson reported two shots lodged in his foremast, one in the foreyard, and two in the mainmast. But if they did not bring down a stick, the gunners of the privateer cut the ship's rigging to pieces. Four main-shrouds, one main-topmast backstay and five fore-shrouds were shot away. Later the captain of the *Crow Castle* reported one hundred and forty-two shot holes in her sails, two shots through her hull on the starboard quarter, and many balls sticking in her sides. Despite this, no gun was dismounted, nor a British seaman killed or wounded. They still were able to serve their weapons and keep the *Black Princess* at bay.

After an hour and a half of vain efforts to close, Macatter decided to call it off. He had suffered only superficially, but he cared to risk no longer the fire of an enemy he could not board. His purpose was prizes, but not at the expense of too much damage from a quarry offering such formidable resistance. To be disabled so far from a friendly port might be disastrous. So he sheered off, heading for the brig astern, and smarting under the disappointment. Behind him the crew of the *Crow Castle* strove to get up sail and go to their consort's assistance. This valiant effort was futile, however, as the privateer's guns had left the ship with "hardly a running rope whole."

The *Black Princess*' next intended victim was another *John,* a lightly armed brig, Captain Rawson, from Memel for Whitehaven. Rawson had been alarmed by the attack upon the *Crow Castle,* and had sought safety in flight. But his brig was a slow sailer and was quickly overhauled. When he saw escape impossible, the British captain pluckily opened fire.

Having been frustrated once that Sunday evening, Macatter was not to be beaten off again. He closed in rapidly until abreast of the brig, and gave her a devastating broadside. This time his guns were better served, or the shots were luckier than during the encounter with the ship. One ball struck Rawson, shattering an elbow. Its force hurled him off his feet and down the scuttle. His crew presumed him dead, and, when a second broadside wounded the mate in the thigh and killed a seaman, they had had enough. Down came the *John*'s flag.

The boarding party was headed by Macatter, whose conduct, if the enemy's account is to be credited, was strangely at variance with his accustomed civility. No doubt

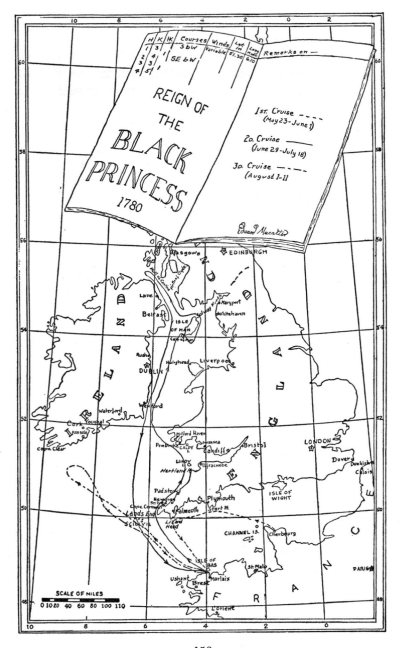

REIGN OF
THE
BLACK
PRINCESS
1780

1st. Cruise - - - -
(May 23-June 1)

2d. Cruise ———
(June 29-July 18)

3d. Cruise — — —
(August 1-11)

| H | K | K | Courses | Winds | Lat. in | Long. in | Remarks on — |
|---|---|---|---------|-------|---------|----------|--------------|
| 1 | 3 |   | S b W | Variable | 57.30 | 6.10 | |
| 2 | 4 | 1 | | | | | |
| 3 | 3 | 1 | SE b W | | | | |
| 4 | 5 | 1 | | | | | |

pique over his earlier failure explains it in part, or, perhaps, the British version was highly colored. Rawson was in his cabin, where he had been carried from the foot of the scuttle. His wounds were badly in need of dressing, but help was refused him although the cutter's surgeon had come on board to treat the mate and one or two wounded men. Instead, as the story was told from an unfriendly source, Macatter used "the most diabolical language to him for having dared to defend himself, and threatened to burn the ship with the crew in her, if he did not submit to such terms for ransom as the villain dictated." Maybe it was all true. More probably, not. The only certainty is that Rawson agreed to a thousand pound ransom. A hostage was taken on board the *Black Princess,* and the *John* was left to be joined by the *Crow Castle,* which, by then, had managed to get up some sail and was bearing down.[3]

The *Black Princess* continued her northward foray, and next day, south of McArthur's Head, on the island of Islay, added two more prizes. One was a small sloop from Christiansand for Greenock; the other, a ship from Memel to Clyde. Both were ransomed. After that, Macatter turned south, sailing unmolested through the North Channel, the Irish Sea, and St. George's Channel, to arrive in Morlaix on July 18. He brought in twenty-six ransomers for a total of £10,500, representing twenty-six prizes taken in a cruise of but twenty days!

Sixteen prisoners delivered by the *Black Princess* and

3 How deceptive appearances and reports may be is evidenced by the account of an eyewitness who watched from a promontory near Larne, Ireland: "On Sunday evening a ship was seen engaged with a brig and cutter in the Channel, off the Mull of Cantyre, and in a short time the cutter sheered off leaving the ship and brig engaged, who soon closed, and from the firing ceasing, it is presumed one of them struck to the other. . . ." The London *Chronicle,* July 20–22, 1780. The cutter seen sheering off was, of course, the *Black Princess,* which had just taken and ransomed the *John.*

two previously arrived in the *Padmore* were available for exchange. The commissary proposed sending them off in a cartel which had just brought one hundred French prisoners into Morlaix. Macatter and John Diot protested vigorously. They recalled the fifty or more Britishers Franklin had released at M. de Sartine's request the previous winter and for whom no Americans had been returned from England. The captain sent a remonstrance, too, to Passy.

"The Uncertainty of their being to be Exchanged here for Americans," Macatter wrote, "has induced me to Request from the Commissary that they Should not be Sent off, until fresh Orders be issued from Your Excellency for their fate." He added emphatically, that, "and I would like Rather to maintain 'em in Gaol at my Own Expences, than to have 'em lost for the Congress."

While remaining time for his cruise was short, he prophesied he would make it good and bring in enough additional prisoners to warrant a cartel to exchange Americans only. If Franklin did not uphold him, he warned that "not one single man wou'd go any more to Sea with me." He would prove he was not undeserving of the Doctor's support, and would do so "at the risk of my Life and bottom." The "bottom," not to be misunderstood, was the *Black Princess*.[4]

Two weeks were required for repairs. While she lay at Morlaix dock, London papers jubilantly proclaimed that the *Black Princess* had been taken off Land's End on July 28—and without a shot being fired—by a frigate, brig, and cutter in His Majesty's service. That was amusing reading for Macatter, who sailed from Bas Road on August 1, and headed right for the locality where report had it he already had been taken.

4 This letter of Macatter's, in Franklin Papers, APS, seems to be the only one preserved.

Within four days he intercepted and ransomed six vessels, and determined to send in a seventh prize, the brig *Enterprize*—from Liverpool to Plymouth with coal, rum, earthenware, and cheese. William Ripner, who previously had carried in the *Padmore,* was placed in the *Enterprize* with a prize crew and headed for France. Two Guernsey privateers chased him close in with the coast of Brittany, and forced him to run into a small port ten leagues west of Morlaix.

The *Black Princess,* meanwhile, headed for the Irish coast. South of Cape Clear the brig *St. Joseph,* outward bound from Waterford for Newfoundland, was picked up on August 9, sixteen hours after she had started her voyage. She had a valuable cargo of merchandise, and Macatter decided to keep her in company and make for home. He had six hostages and eighteen prisoners on board, and the cruising period for which the crew had signed on was growing short. He returned—bringing his prize in with him— on Friday night, August 11.

News of the arrival of the *Enterprize, St. Joseph,* and the cutter herself at Morlaix reached London, to refute previous claims that the Irish-manned scourge had been taken. Newspaper editors confessed sadly that "the reports of the Black Princess privateer being captured is premature." [5]

[5] The London *Chronicle,* August 19–22, 1780, announced the capture of the *Black Princess* by the *Aurora* frigate and her consorts. The London *Courant,* August 18, admitted the report unfounded, and added that the privateer had taken two prizes since her supposed capture.

## CHAPTER XV

# *Second Cruise of the* Fearnot

DEPARTURE OF THE *Fearnot* from Dunkirk had been much delayed. When John Torris had reported to Franklin in June that Ryan would shortly continue his cruise, the merchant and his Irish captain reckoned without their M. de Sartine. Just when the cutter was ready to sail with a crew of whom one-third were Frenchmen, the Minister of Marine unexpectedly raided the port for seamen for the Royal navy. An order arrived June 20, to inspect every privateer in the harbor and remove all French hands. Some seven hundred seamen were gathered in that day. Merchants talked wrathfully of a memorial to the King, protesting a breach of promise by M. de Sartine, whose promptings when the war began had led them to risk their property in such adventures.

While the *Fearnot* was crippled, she did not suffer as much as many privateers, whose crews had been solidly Frenchmen. It was bad enough, though, and entailed a two weeks' delay before Ryan could replace the men he had lost to the Royal impress. He never quite filled the gaps. When he sailed about July 8, his complement was around eighty, some dozen or more fewer than the number on board for the first cruise. Regardless of this handicap, his destination was the same as before—northward around the top of Scotland. There he could prey upon the trade from the Baltic and from Canada for the west coast ports of Scotland and Ireland.

No prizes marked his progress up along England's eastern shore. Off Buchan Ness, a promontory midway between Aberdeen and Fraserburgh, on July 12, he stopped and searched a brig. She was the *Elizabeth and Peggy,* from Christiansand for Stromness in the Orkneys, with a cargo of deals. Unfortunately for Ryan, she previously had been taken and ransomed by a French privateer. While the vessel was thus immune, not so her crew. The cutter's hands "plundered her of almost everything they could get belonging to the Master or men." [1]

No more merchantmen were encountered as the *Fearnot* passed to the north of Scotland. Pentland Firth, separating the main from the Orkneys, was barren of sail. Rounding Cape Wrath and veering southward into the North Minch, Ryan appeared in Stornoway Harbor, on the island of Lewis in the outer Hebrides, on the afternoon of July 24. Consternation seized the little town as a warning gun from the *Fearnot* was followed by the landing of a boatload of Irishmen with their redoubtable captain in the sternsheets. The inhabitants of Stornoway were defenseless. Back in 1745, the islanders had rallied to the cause of the Young Pretender. Parliament had retaliated the following year by ordering them disarmed. Consequently they now had no weapons of any description and "were at the mercy

[1] The master of the *Elizabeth and Peggy* made an affidavit at Stromness in July, which is most confusing. He related his capture by a French privateer, and his subsequent meeting with the *Fearnot.* Then he concluded: "On the 15th current he fell in with Paul Jones, as Commodore of three frigates with a number of men on board them, Buchaness then bearing W. and by N. about 12 leagues distant, when the vessel was plundered a second time, and all their clothes, liquors, and 10 s. in silver taken from the crew." The London *Chronicle,* August 3–5, 1780. As Jones at that time was in L'Orient preparing the frigate *Ariel* for a voyage to America, he must have been impersonated by someone on board the frigates, which, unquestionably, were French.

of every boat's crew the enemy might chuse to send on shore."

Some of the leading citizens assembled fearfully at the main wharf as Ryan stepped from the boat. He knew their plight and lost no time in demanding a sizable ransom, backed by a threat to burn the town and the shipping in the harbor unless there was immediate compliance. Such accounts as are available do not specify the amount of money he required, but agree it was "a very heavy contribution." The residents could not raise the sum immediately. Several offered themselves as security if Ryan would spare the town, promising the ransom would be paid later. The captain agreed, and called in his boat's crew, which had scattered for a bit of plundering. What loot they carried away with them when they put back to the *Fearnot* the record does not state. Toward dusk, the privateer sailed off bearing "some of the principal inhabitants hostages."

Some fifteen miles south of Stornoway at the entrance of Loch Sheil, Ryan added a touch of humor to his progress. He went on board a small sloop to the great alarm of its occupants, a little group of gentlemen from Londonderry in Ireland, "who had come a pleasuring to the Highlands." There was one alien figure among them—the laird of a nearby estate, who had joined the party from the shore. He was attired in full regalia of bonnet and kilts, and was the first to remonstrate when he learned they were being taken by an American privateer.

In broad Scotch dialect, he protested that the Irish gentlemen were on a fishing trip and shortly would join him upon his estate for a wee bit of hunting. Surely the American captain would not disturb them in their pleasure. In fact, should the captain but deign to accompany them, he would be delighted to entertain him as well. Not to be outdone in courtesy, Ryan assumed his best French manners. He was a sportsman, too, he replied, but did not, however, explain that his sportsmanship had been the lively and wary activity of a poacher in county Dublin. He could well understand their disappointment in being so rudely interrupted. Far be it from him, however, to spoil their vacation. He would ask for a modest ransom, he said, and would not permit either his officers or men to land on the laird's estate, for he could not prevent plundering when they were ashore.

Such consideration charmed the bonneted Scotch gentleman, who felt he had been treated "in the most agreeable and genteelest manner that I could expect from an enemy." He and his Irish friends had funds with them to pay the ransom in cash, and avoid the unpleasant necessity of surrendering one of their number as a hostage. Ryan bowed himself over the side and left them to their "pleasuring." He sallied out of Loch Sheil in pursuit of a ship, which proved to be from Liverpool and his first worthwhile prize. He ransomed her for a sizable sum.[2]

From the outer, he turned his attention to the inner Hebrides. The Liverpool ship had been intercepted midway in the Minch, which the *Fearnot* crossed on a course almost due south. By dusk of July 27, the north shore of the island of Skye had been reached. Before the short northern night set in, they picked up the sailors' landmark of "The Old Man," a tall pinnacle in the Storr. Guided by it, they made their way into Raasay Sound. An hour later, the cutter arrived off Portree, principal town on Skye. Ryan heralded his approach by a discharge of musket shots. A sloop loaded with meal was boarded and ransomed. Another, with salt and casks, was run ashore and

2 The humorous tale of the Scotch laird's encounter with Ryan is told in a letter "from a Gentleman at Stornaway to his Friend at Edinburgh, dated August 14 [1780]." It appeared in the London *Chronicle*, September 5–7, 1780. Other accounts of the early activities of the *Fearnot* during this second cruise are in the London *Courant*, August 16, and the London *Chronicle*, August 12–15, 1780.

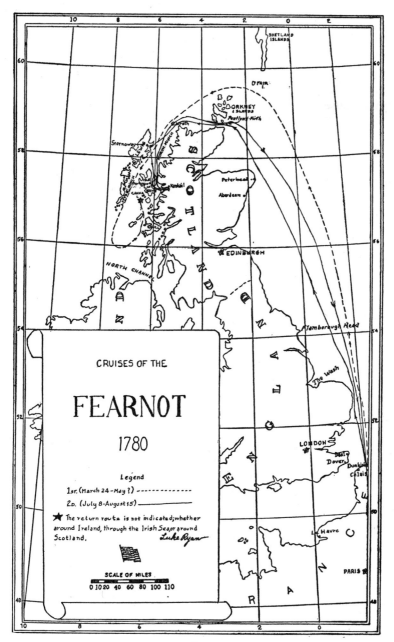

CRUISES OF THE

# FEARNOT

## 1780

Legend

1st. (March 24 – May ?) ------------

2d. (July 8 – August 15) ————————

★ The return route is not indicated; whether around Ireland, through the Irish Sea or around Scotland.

*Luke Ryan*

SCALE OF MILES

0 10 20 40 60 80 100 110

deserted by her master and crew. The privateersmen pulled her off. Her owner had remained on board. Ryan was favorable to him, as the story was told, "on account of civilities formerly shewn him, he having been entertained at the gentleman's house the week before." Whatever the reason, the sloop was liberated.

Portree's population had spent a fearful and uncomfortable night. They, too, were destitute of arms and expected to be pillaged. At dawn they were happily disappointed. Instead of levying a ransom, Ryan sent ashore a request to buy mutton and beef. Moreover, when he was supplied with "sixteen wethers and three stots"— lambs and steers in the Highland dialect—he astounded the townsfolk by paying ready money for them. Why Portree escaped the fate of Stornoway, he left unexplained.

Continuing south in Raasay Sound on July 29, they took a small vessel in ballast lying in Loch Sligachan. Her crew had deserted her, so they removed her masts, sails, and some of her gear. Then they proceeded toward the Kyle, a channel scarcely a quarter-mile wide, separating the mainland from Skye. In the Kyle they came upon and ransomed a brig bound out for Inverkeithing, a port in the Firth of Forth. For reasons best known to himself, and disclosed to no one, Ryan pushed on through Loch Alsh and Loch Duich to the town of Kintail, thus penetrating a dozen miles into the Scotch main before he decided to retrace his course. His crew landed at that hamlet, and celebrated this furthest invasion of enemy land by plundering the public house to the tune of eighty guineas.

Now homeward bound, the *Fearnot* returned through the Kyle and veered northward up the Inner Sound between the island of Raasay and the Scotch shore. Her passage was marked by capture of eight more vessels. Five were ransomed. Three were burned, and their crews put ashore. By August 2, Ryan was back in the Minch. Behind him loud complaints arose against the Ministry, which had kept them defenseless for thirty years. "Scarce a day passes without his making a descent upon some part of the coast, carrying away the cattle, or plundering the houses of the wretched inhabitants," cried a gentleman who spoke with more venom than veracity. "We are in a sad situation here," wailed another, "as we are not entrusted with a single musket to defend ourselves." "Government alone is able to relieve us from this dilemma," was one statement with which all were in agreement.[3]

The cause of all these diatribes, meanwhile, was on his way north about, with fourteen hostages on board, but not a prisoner. His excuses were the usual ones—too small a crew to send off prizes, too little room on board, too many mouths to feed for a long period of time, and too far away from a home port. Undetected, and with no further incidents, Luke Ryan set his course for Dunkirk, and arrived safely in mid-August. Franklin learned of his return and wrote to John Torris: "I congratulate you on the success I hear Capt. Ryan has lately had, and wish you a continuance of Good Fortune." [4]

[3] A gentleman signing himself Mercator, and writing from Inverness on August 4, 1780, opened his complaint against government failure to protect them from the enemy with the statement: "On the west coast the Fearnought American privateer, Luke Ryan, commander, reigns uncontrolled." London *Chronicle,* August 19–22, 1780.

[4] This, Franklin's last reference to the *Fearnot,* is the concluding sentence of a letter to Torris of August 23, 1780. It is in Letter Books, 1780.

Chapter XVI

# The Adventure Ends

THE FRENCH COURT took better than a month to weigh Franklin's reasons for having issued American commissions to French-owned privateers, having acted as Judge of the Admiralty for their prizes, and having condemned the *Flora*'s cargo. Even then, its determination extended no further than what should be done about the complaint from the Ambassador of Holland. This decision M. de Vergennes conveyed to the Doctor on July 24. Franklin's offer to recall the commissions for the *Black Prince* and *Black Princess* had been considered, the French Minister wrote. While not empowered at that time to demand such action, he would, nevertheless, advise it. However, said he, the King wished that the case of the Dutch ship should be brought before the Council of Prizes where it would be judged according to the laws and rules established for the French privateers.

"I acquiesce in it with pleasure," Franklin replied next day. Still vexed by the way M. de Sartine's bland refusal to accept any responsibility had placed him in an unfavorable light with the French Court, Franklin felt it highly desirable to reaffirm to M. de Vergennes, that, if he had acted improperly, he had just and ample excuses.

"I had the honor of acquainting your Excellency in mine

of the 18th past with the motives urged to me for granting
an American Commission to the Black Prince," the Doctor continued. "Afterwards I was, without seeking or desiring it, drawn into the exercise of a kind of judicial power
respecting her prizes by being assured that your tribunals
refused to judge of prizes made by American cruisers, and
by being shown the eleventh article of the King's regula-
tion of September 27, 1778, directing the officers of the
Admiralty to send me copies of all their proceedings and
the papers relating to any prize brought into your ports by
such cruisers, which it was alleged was intended to enable
me to judge of the legality of these prizes, which judgment
was therefore demanded of me."

For proof, he selected a note addressed to him by the
Minister of Marine the previous September, and inserted
it in the letter. M. de Sartine at that time had forwarded
him procès-verbaux upon nine prizes with the comment
that the Council of Prizes had not judged itself competent to pass upon them; which note, Franklin remarked,
"seemed to confirm this." And he thought to himself, it
should help also to show Vergennes the duplicity of the
Minister of Marine. In conclusion, the Doctor told the
Foreign Minister, he would act upon his advice, which,
after all, amounted to a virtual command, and "withdraw
the only two commissions I have issued to the privateers
fitted out by the King's subjects." [1]

By that statement, Franklin was guilty of a bit of deception also. He had issued four commissions—not two—
namely: one to Stephen Marchant for the *Black Prince,*
dated May 19, 1779; one to Patrick Dowlin for the same
cutter, on October 15, 1779; another, of the like date, to

[1] Franklin's letter of July 25, 1780 is printed in Wharton (ed.), *Revolu
tionary Diplomatic Correspondence,* III, 880, 881, but not the letter from
Vergennes which provoked it. The latter is in "Letters in French, 1778–
1780," Franklin Papers, Library of Congress.

Edward Macatter for the *Black Princess;* and one to Luke
Ryan, on February 4, 1780, for the *Fearnot.* To be sure,
two of these were for the same vessel, and as she had been
lost, only the commissions for the *Black Princess* and *Fearnot* remained in force. The Doctor's studied avoidance of
any mention of the *Fearnot* in his correspondence with
Vergennes, or, for that matter, with Congress, he left unexplained. His promise to withdraw "the only two commissions I have issued" would leave much to conjecture. But
in his visits to Versailles he had learned enough about the
*Fearnot* to refrain from any written comments about her.

When the first complaint regarding the *Flora* reached
the French Court, M. de Sartine had been ordered to review all papers for privateers owned by Torris and operating under the American flag. He had begun with the *Fearnot* and had found in her contract terms "so contrary to
regulations," that he professed amazement that the Dunkirk Admiralty had permitted registration of the privateer.
He had then informed M. Chardon that it was the King's
will that the contract be suppressed. By the time the latter
took action, Ryan had sailed on his second cruise. The
clause to which M. de Sartine took objection, and which
he later found in the contracts for the *Black Prince* and
*Black Princess,* was a renunciation by the subscribers of all
benefits guaranteed "by all ordinances and regulations of
the marine which are contrary to the said contract." Inas-
much as the Minister of Marine's action upon the *Fearnot*
had been taken in the previous May, Franklin regarded
the affairs of that privateer closed, and saw no need to
discuss them further.[2]

2 The case of the *Fearnot* is discussed at some length by Henry Malo
in his "American Privateers at Dunkerque," but his deductions from
what he gleaned from the French Admiralty Records for Dunkirk are
not accurate. He assumed that Torris "sought to escape from the jurisdiction of the Admiralty, to which he of course was subject, by submitting
his prizes to the judgment of foreign courts and thus renouncing the

John Torris' reaction to the cancellation of the commissions was as the Doctor expected. The merchant prepared a memorial and handed it to the intendant at Dunkirk to be transmitted to M. de Sartine, "Showing the Dangerous Consequences attending to the Armateur, & nay to the State, the Withdrawing the American Commission to our Black Princess, & that, at any rate, there is an impossibility of recalling it untill her three months Cruise are out." She was still at sea, he continued in his explanation to Franklin, and " 'Twould be most injust & ungenerous to all, & nay it is utterly Impossible to recall her Commission before her Three months Cruise are finisht."

In brief acknowledgment on August 7, Franklin told Torris he hoped there would be a favorable answer to the memorial, and that he would endeavor to promote it at Versailles. He had condemned Macatter's prize, the *Padmore,* and the judgment already had been forwarded to Morlaix, he continued. Judgments upon the ransoms for the May cruise were being sent to the Admiralty Court there that same day. Procès-verbaux on the ransoms for the July cruise had not yet reached him at Passy, but he wanted to compliment the merchant upon the late successes of the *Black Princess.*

Franklin already had voiced appreciation of Macatter's achievements to the captain himself in a warmly worded letter praising his activity and bravery. "I see by the English News Papers," the Doctor had written, "that you have much alarmed the Enemy's Coasts, and done great Damage to their Commerce, your bringing in so many Prisoners is another considerable service, and you may depend on having your generous Intentions fulfilled in the Exchange and

---

authority of his own sovereign." Malo makes it sound like a heinous crime, whereas the French Court and the French Admiralty had connived in Franklin's efforts until the taking of the Dutch ship *Flora* brought complaints from a neutral power.

Deliverance of so many Americans." He reassured Macatter that the prisoners definitely would be exchanged for them, and not for Frenchmen. The Britishers safely could be put on board the cartel ship, and a receipt taken, "that they were on account of America." Franklin did not advise the captain, however, that the reward awaiting him at Dunkirk upon completion of his cruise would be withdrawal of his American commission.[3]

Writing to Congress on August 10, Franklin omitted any mention that his privateers were nearing the end of their course. But he did not fail to extol their accomplishments; in fact, he indulged in some slight exaggeration, thus:

> The Privateers Black Prince and Black Princess, with Congress commissions issued here by me and manned partly with Americans, have greatly harassed the English coasting trade, having taken in eighteen months near one hundred and twenty sail. The Prince was wrecked on this coast; the men saved. The Princess still reigns, and in a late cruise of twenty days between June 20 and July 10 took twenty-eight prizes, some very valuable.[4]

For the first time in his correspondence with Congress, he said nothing about his efforts in behalf of the prisoners in England. His latest rebuffs momentarily had discouraged him. Word had come from William Hodgson that the Commissioners of Sick and Hurt were still adamant in refusing to exchange Americans for Britishers taken by the French in lieu of those delivered up in Holland, and continued in their determination not to honor paroles at sea.

3 John Torris' letter of protest against the loss of the American commissions is in Franklin Papers, APS. Franklin's reply, and his letter to Macatter, are in Letter Books, 1780.

4 The paragraph in Franklin's letter of August 10, 1780 was his last public utterance to Congress regarding his privateering activities. It is published in Wharton (ed.), *Revolutionary Diplomatic Correspondence,* IV, 25, 26.

Hodgson had drawn up a memorial to the Lords of the Admiralty, but had small hope of success. What progress had been made in negotiations seemed to have been nullified by the empty cartel from Morlaix. Even M. de Sartine's belated admission that the blunder was of French origin had not mollified their Lordships. Altogether, Franklin had no news upon the subject of prisoners to give to Congress, and, in his characteristic manner, having nothing to say, kept silent.

On the same day that his dispatch left Passy for America, an edict under the hand of Louis XVI put an end to his services as a judge of the Admiralty. He learned about it three days later from M. de Vergennes. The Foreign Minister enclosed a copy of a letter from the King to the Duke de Penthievre, High Admiral of France, "concerning the future judgment of prizes brought in by the privateers fitted out in France under commissions from Congress."

Franklin perused the letter. Difficulties had arisen, the King stated, as to the proper jurisdiction over such prizes. To end all doubts, hereafter they would be judged by the Council for Prizes in the same manner as the Council judged those sent in by vessels bearing French commissions. The officers of the Admiralty should observe the formalities prescribed in the King's declaration of June 24, 1778, and no longer be governed by the regulations of the subsequent September. Notification should be sent to all ports, "so that the capt$^s$. of those privateers as well as the officers of the Admiralty may be informed thereof & Act conformably." [5]

[5] A translation of this letter by Charles Thomson, secretary of the Continental Congress, is in the Papers of the Continental Congress, 37, 341. Another translation was printed in the London *Chronicle*, September 16–19, 1780. Vergennes' covering letter of August 13, 1780, is not in Wharton, but exists in the "Letters in French, 1778–1780" in the Franklin Papers, Library of Congress.

M. de Vergennes's covering note asked whether, as he had suggested on July 24, Franklin had yet withdrawn the commissions for the *Black Prince* and *Black Princess?* The decision of the French Court was most welcome. It relieved the Doctor of duties he had never sought and which were becoming more onerous and daily less useful to the United States. He had assumed responsibility as a judge of the Admiralty because it had been a necessary part of his main objective—the exchange of American prisoners. True, from the spectacular viewpoint of preying upon and greatly alarming the British trade his venture into privateering had been eminently successful. Results had enriched the pockets of John Torris, if not those of the Irish captains, and the crew members, and had made good reading in letters to Congress.

But he had not accomplished what he had fondly hoped for—the bringing in of an abundance of British prisoners to redeem his own countrymen from long and painful captivity. The British Admiralty's continued refusal to accept sea paroles and its insistence upon exchanging Americans only for Britishers taken by vessels under American commission, had made it more and more imperative that the privateers bring in their captives. Yet, in all the cruises of the *Black Prince, Black Princess,* and *Fearnot* only one hundred and sixty-one prisoners had arrived in French ports.

He asked Temple to cast up the net results—the Doctor admitting to a distaste for figures. It showed that, of the prisoners brought in, twenty-four had enlisted in the privateers and five were released as neutrals (the crew of the *Flora*), leaving one hundred and thirty-two for exchange. But ten prizes had been recaptured with prize crews totaling thirty-seven. The net gain was ninety-five, which Franklin admitted was a disappointing result from eighteen months of cruising.

The long hours of tedious conning over procès-verbaux, the interminable correspondence with the French Court, Admiralty officers, John Torris and the captains, and the high postage cost for all the voluminous documents, from port to Passy and Passy to port, made the whole privateering effort, judged by the goal he had set, one that he was truly glad to abandon. Getting the American prisoners in England released would continue to be his purpose, but he saw that it would require other means than French-owned, American-commissioned privateers.

Likewise, during the past nine months, he had become sickened with maritime affairs which had thrust themselves upon him. They were consuming valuable hours that he could better have spent on pressing matters of state. These affairs were aftermaths of John Paul Jones's brilliant cruise: the charges against Peter Landais, French captain of the *Alliance;* the inquiry at Passy into those charges, requiring days of interrogation of the half-mad Frenchman; and the subsequent seizure of the *Alliance* by Landais at L'Orient, in direct disobedience to the Doctor's orders. Added to that, Franklin had discovered that he had had to act as Judge of the Admiralty for Jones's prizes, the *Bonhomme Richard* having been commissioned in France, and not American owned. That had forced him to peruse, as well, the procès-verbal for the *Serapis, Countess of Scarborough,* and several merchantmen. Altogether, it was just too much for the gout-ridden Minister Plenipotentiary.

A score or more of procès-verbaux upon the prizes taken by Macatter in his latest cruise had just come to hand. Franklin turned them over to Temple, instructing him to wrap them up and deliver them to the Council of Prizes. Then he acknowledged Vergennes's letter. "I have written to the owners of the Black Prince and Princess recalling their commissions," he informed the Foreign Minister. "The answer I have received is, that the Black Prince is wrecked upon the coast, and her commission therefore void; that the Princess is out upon a cruise, and that as soon as the cruise is finished her commission can be obtained from the government to continue acting under it, which the owners say they have applied for." This latter statement is not expressed with Franklin's usual clarity, or else his secretary, Lair De Lamotte, transcribed it carelessly in entering it in the legation letter book. The latter was probably the case, young Lamotte quite often being guilty of sentences more involved than Franklin's precise English. The concluding words to Vergennes, however, were terse and clear; "I have no other interest in those armaments than the advantage of some prisoners to exchange for my countrymen."

A week elapsed before Franklin conveyed to John Torris the final decision of the court. He told the merchant he believed the shipping of French seamen as well as the taking of the *Flora* had contributed to raising the alarm against him. Franklin had in mind, of course, the fifteen sailors of the Royal navy Macatter had shipped at night in the harbor of Cherbourg for his second cruise. If the captains in future abstained from such infringements of the laws of the land, the Doctor assumed they would be able to continue in their respective commands with French commissions. For the future their prizes would be judged by the Council of Prizes. He was through; was absolved of all connections with them hereafter, but he wished them "a continuance of Good Fortune."

There was a bit of recompense in the appreciation voiced in John Torris' acknowledgment. Macatter had arrived at Dunkirk from Morlaix, the *Black Princess* having had an uneventful run up the Channel. She was preparing for sea and the merchant had applied for a French commission. The captain certainly would obey Franklin's suggestions, and, wrote Torris, "We are both gratefull for all your Excellency's favours."

Despite all Franklin's regrets, the accomplishments of his privateers he realized had been phenomenal. The *Black Prince* alone had taken thirty-five prizes; the *Black Princess,* forty-three; the two cruising in consort, twenty; and the *Fearnot,* sixteen. The grand total was one hundred and fourteen British vessels of all descriptions sent in, burned, scuttled, or ransomed. And these desperate Irishmen throughout all their cruising had defied capture, beating off the King's cutters in every encounter.

Better than that, however, had been the consternation of British shipowners, the soaring of marine insurance rates, the havoc to the coastal trade in the English, Irish, and Scotch seas, and the discomfiture of the British Admiralty. No other raiders, save John Paul Jones, struck heavier blows at British pride as "Mistress of the Seas" than Dr. Franklin's little privateers, with their hardened crews of Irish smugglers.

# Epilogue

D<small>ESPITE THE FATE</small> which might await them if taken under the flag of France, all of Franklin's Irish captains accepted French commissions, and sailed in privateers armed by John Torris. The Doctor followed their adventures through the ensuing years of the war. Two of them came to grief. Luke Ryan was taken in April, 1781, and Edward Macatter six months later. Both were tried before the High Court of Admiralty in the Old Bailey on March 30, 1782, and convicted of "Felony and Piracy on the High Seas," despite Ryan's efforts to prove himself a native of France, and Macatter's insistence that he had been born in Boston. Their hanging on Execution Dock was set for May 14. But they were respited, first for fourteen days, and then until "his Majesty's further Orders." Belatedly the French Court interceded and, as the North Ministry had fallen, and a more tolerant administration was at the helm, a pardon eventually was granted each captain.

Meanwhile, John Torris, considering his two captains as doomed, refused to admit that he owed them any money, claiming non-receipt of the proceeds of the prizes they had taken under both American and French commissions. Macatter's wife appealed to Franklin, and Ryan, once released and back in France, petitioned the French Court as he could "expect no Justis from the praeincibles of my Eagent John Torris." Their efforts failed, as Torris had gone into bankruptcy, and also to jail where he remained until 1788.

That same year, Patrick Dowlin, who, after the war, had received a commission in the French navy, was discharged from the service for living "a life of the greatest debauch by passing days and nights in drinking in dens with the worst riff-raff of English sailors, to such a degree that the other lieutenants of the king's frigates at Dunkerque have never wished to have the least relations with him or even see him." What happened to Macatter is not known, but Ryan died in 1789 in the King's Bench Prison in London. He had not received a shilling of the money due to him, amounting to 160,000 livres, and "was confined for a debt of 100 l. at the faculty's suit for the innoculation of three of his children." [1]

Franklin's experience with privateering and the resultant burden thrust upon him remained vividly in his memory to the end of his days. About sixteen months before his death, in enumerating his services to the United States, he dwelt at some length upon the extra duties he had been called upon to perform in France. In one of these, he had acted, he wrote in the third person, "though without any special commission for the purpose, as a judge of the admiralty; for, the Congress having sent him a quantity of blank commissions for privateering, he granted them to cruisers fitted out in the ports of France, some of them manned by old smugglers who knew every creek on the coast of England . . . All the papers taken in each prize brought in, were by virtue of an order of Council sent up to Mr. Franklin, who had to examine them, judge of the

[1] The preliminary hearings, trials, respites and pardons of Luke Ryan and Edward Macatter were painstakingly described in the London newspapers through 1781 and 1782. Of John Torris' defalcation, the evidence comes from Macatter's wife, Mary, and Ryan himself, their letters of September 12, 1782, and August 8, 1784, respectively, being in Franklin Papers, APS. Torris' bankruptcy is described in Henry Malo, "American Privateers at Dunkerque." Ryan's death and a rather garbled account of his privateering exploits appeared in the *Pennsylvania Journal*, Philadelphia, October 7, 1789.

legality of the capture, and write to the admiralty of the port, that he found the prize good, and that the sale might be permitted."

One of these privateers, the *Black Prince*, as he recalled it, had in the course of a year taken seventy-five sail!

Allowance must be made for the failing memory of the grand old octogenarian, who, in December, 1788, could recollect prize-taking and procès-verbal reading, but had forgotten the reason that had prompted him to commission his privateers—his unfortunate countrymen in British prisons.[2]

[2] Franklin prepared the "Sketch of the Services of B. Franklin to the United States of America" at the request of Charles Thomson, and enclosed it in a letter of December 29, 1788. It was first published in the Proceedings of the New York Historical Society, and reprinted in Smyth (ed.), *Writings of Benjamin Franklin*, IX, 691–697.

# *Appendix*

The following tabulation gives a summary of prizes and prisoners taken during the various cruises of Benjamin Franklin's three privateers, in 1779 and 1780.

| Vessels and Cruise | Prizes taken | Lost, Scuttled or Burned | Ransomed | Re-taken | Brought in | Prisoners Paroled | Brought in |
|---|---|---|---|---|---|---|---|
| *Black Prince,* | | | | | | | |
| 1st | 8 | 0 | 1 | 6 | 1 | 0 | 21 |
| 2d | 13 | 0 | 11 | 1 | 1 | 29 | 11 |
| 3d | 8 | 0 | 8 | 0 | 0 | 0 | 2 |
| 4th | 5 | 3 | 1 | 1 | 0 | 5 | 18 |
| 5th | 1 | 0 | 0 | 0 | 1 | 0 | 5 |
| *Black Prince and Black Princess,* | | | | | | | |
| 1st | 13 | 0 | 5 | 2 | 6 | 2 | 68 |
| 2d | 7 | 1 | 3 | 0 | 3 | 21 | 0 |
| *Black Princess,* | | | | | | | |
| 1st | 6 | 0 | 5 | 1 | 0 | 12 | 0 |
| 2d | 29 | 2 | 26 | 0 | 1 | 0 | 18 |
| 3d | 8 | 0 | 6 | 0 | 2 | 0 | 18 |
| *Fearnot,* | | | | | | | |
| 1st | 4 | 1 | 2 | 0 | 1 | 57 | 0 |
| 2d | 12 | 4 | 8 | 0 | 0 | 0 | 0 |
| | 114 | 11 | 76 | 11 | 16 | 126 | 161 |

# Bibliography and Critique

THE BIBLIOGRAPHY OF THIS BOOK is intensive rather than extensive. Some of the material used is in print. Most of it, however, comes from manuscript collections found in public repositories, here or abroad. The great bulk of it, of course, relates to Benjamin Franklin, either letters written by him or to him, or documents prepared for his eyes.

## Published Correspondence, Biography, and Other Writings

Printed material bearing upon Franklin insofar as his privateering activities are concerned is most disappointing. Incomplete collections of Franklin's writings are available. Among those that have appeared in book form are William Temple Franklin (ed.), *Memoirs of the Life and Writings of Benjamin Franklin,* 3 vols. (London, 1818); Jared Sparks (ed.), *The Works of Benjamin Franklin,* 10 vols. (Boston, 1840); John Bigelow (ed.), *The Complete Works of Benjamin Franklin,* 10 vols. (New York, 1887–89); and Albert Henry Smyth (ed.), *The Writings of Benjamin Franklin,* 10 vols. (New York, 1905–07). Naturally, each was an improvement over its predecessor, but even the latest, already a half-century old, is incomplete and totally inadequate. Fortunately, a new edition of Franklin's writings, comprising in- as well as out-letters, is being undertaken. It will, no doubt, embrace practically everything written by and to the Doctor, which today can be found only in manuscript form.

A compilation of letters to and from Franklin while serving as one of the American Commissioners and later as Minister Plenipotentiary to France was edited by Edward Everett Hale and E. E. Hale, Jr., entitled *Franklin in France,* 2 vols. (Boston, 1887–88). The Hales had access to all the various Franklin collections, but their selections were made without discrimination, their editing careless, and their identification of letter writers not always accurate.

Too careful editing of capitalization, punctuation, spelling, and even text, on the other hand, mars Francis Wharton's six volumes, *The Revolutionary Diplomatic Correspondence of the United States* (50th Cong., 1st sess.; H. R. Misc. Doc. 603), Washington, D. C., Government Printing Office, 1889. This editing is surprising, as omissions and alterations in the earlier Jared Sparks *The Diplomatic Correspondence of the American Revolution* (Boston, 1829–30) are severely dealt with in Wharton's preface. Also Wharton suffers from incompleteness— printing but half of certain correspondence although the other half was available in the collections he consulted. Perhaps the best example of this is the exchange of letters with M. de Vergennes, the French Minister of Foreign Affairs, regarding the Dutch ship *Flora,* and the French Court's decision to end privateering by French-owned, American-commissioned vessels. Wharton prints three letters on these subjects from Franklin to Vergennes; June 18, July 25, and August 15, 1780. Each letter specifies that it is in reply to a communication of a given date from Vergennes; June 17, July 24, and August 13. These latter three were in a manuscript collection that was then readily available to Wharton in the Department of State. Their omission, of course, has compelled students of the diplomatic correspondence of the period to seek to deduce from Franklin's replies what Vergennes had written.

By an occasional footnote, it is apparent that Wharton was familiar with the American Legation Letter Books then in the Department of State, yet he seemingly used these for reference purposes only. Consequently, he omitted a wealth of letters pertaining to Franklin's privateers. It cannot be claimed that this was because such letters did not relate to diplomacy, for one letter, written on February 9, 1780, to Patrick Dowlin, captain of the *Black Prince,* appears in Wharton's third volume (491, 492), and stands out strikingly as unrelated to anything preceding or following it. The diplomatic correspondence of the period is in need of re-editing as badly as is the Franklin correspondence.

Various biographies of Franklin—from James Parton, *The*

*Life and Times of Benjamin Franklin,* 2 vols. (New York, 1864) to Carl Van Doren, *Benjamin Franklin* (New York, 1938)—are most disappointing on the subject of the Doctor's privateering activities. They contribute little to that topic and disclose an ignorance of what motivated him in that field. Van Doren states that among Franklin's extra-curricular occupations was that of Judge of the Admiralty, and that he condemned prizes taken by American privateers which he had commissioned. However, according to Van Doren, Franklin found this troublesome and exhausting "in part because he disapproved of the whole system." Van Doren discusses and dismisses the subject in about fifty words.

One printed source is of some importance; an article by Henry Malo, "American Privateers at Dunkerque," translated by Stewart L. Mims and published in United States Naval Institute *Proceedings* (No. 139, Vol. 37, No. 3, Annapolis, September, 1911). Malo reaches the amusing conclusion that Dowlin, Ryan, Macatter, and others were Americans. In addition, he is not aware that Benjamin Franklin had any part in the privateering. His value lies in printing several documents from the Dunkirk Archives which throw considerable light upon some of the proceedings in that port, notably the withdrawal of the commission of the *Fearnot,* and the agreement of owners and agent for the joint cruise of the *Black Prince* and *Black Princess.*

### Documents and General Histories

Of lesser value to this study, but useful for comparative purposes is the volume of that excellent British naval historian, Captain W. M. James, C.B., R.N., *The British Navy in Adversity* (London, 1926). James traces the movements of the Grand Fleet with a precision which verifies accounts of specific encounters of Franklin's captains with it.

Gardner W. Allen, *A Naval History of the American Revolution,* 2 vols. (Boston, 1913), utilizing the works of Wharton and Henry Malo, and two Boston newspapers, has touched upon the significance of Franklin's privateering activities, but with no knowledge of the part played by Irish smugglers, or of the persistence with which the Doctor strove to repatriate his countrymen in British prisons.

Mention should be made also of Worthington Chauncey Ford (comp.), *List of the Benjamin Franklin Papers in the Library of Congress,* Washington, D. C., Government Printing Office, 1905, because too often it has been considered as a complete calendar of the Franklin Papers in that repository. It lists but three letters bearing upon Franklin's privateers, and all three are printed in full in Wharton.

Tidbits of information came from two reports of the Historical Manuscript Commission of Great Britain—*The Manuscripts of the Earl of Dartmouth* (Fourteenth Report, Appendix, Part X), 4 vols. (London, 1895), and *Report of the Manuscripts of Mrs. Stopford-Sackville of Drayton House, Northamptonshire* (Ninth Report, Appendix III), 2 vols. (London, 1904–10)—and also from Charles Herbert, *A Relic of the Revolution* (Boston, 1847).

## Newspapers

British newspapers from 1779 to 1782, particularly the London *Chronicle,* London *Courant,* London *Evening Post,* and the London *Public Advertiser,* provide much about the cruises and captures of the privateers, as well as considerable about some of the Irish smugglers who participated in them. Two Boston newspapers, the *Continental Journal* and the *Independent Chronicle,* in their issues of March 9, 1780, provided the only accounts of the *Black Prince* printed contemporaneously in America. In the Newport *Rhode Island Republican,* June 5 and 12, 1839, appeared John Trevett's tribute to the prowess of Luke Ryan.

## Manuscripts and Manuscript Collections

Manuscript sources have provided the great mass of the material utilized, with the American Philosophical Society, Philadelphia, and the Library of Congress sharing equal honors in contributing important letters. With but few exceptions the in-letters are from the former. In the Franklin Papers in the Society, relating to the privateers, are twenty-seven letters from John Torris, nine from Francis Coffyn, eleven from John Diot, nine from Stephen Marchant, seven from William Hodgson, three apiece from Luke Ryan and Patrick Dowlin, and one from Edward Macatter. From lesser characters, who have appeared occasionally in these pages, are letters too numerous to mention.

In the Library of Congress, the Henry Stevens Collection of Franklin Papers includes the American Legation Letter Books for 1779 and 1780, and another letter book, labeled "Letters in French, 1778–1780," which contains contemporary copies of the letters to Franklin written by various French ministers. In this latter volume are all of the letters to Franklin from M. de Vergennes, and M. de Sartine, pertaining to the privateers—their cruises, captures, and final abolishment. None of these have hitherto been printed. In the American Legation Letter Books are contemporary copies of forty-three letters from Franklin, relating to the privateers, which have never appeared in print. These include fifteen to John Torris, eight to M. de Sartine, six to Francis Coffyn, three to John Diot, two each to Luke Ryan and Stephen Marchant, and one to Edward Macatter.

Minutes taken by the register of marine at Morlaix—the procès-verbal which so annoyed Franklin—are in the Franklin Papers in the University of Pennsylvania Library, Philadelphia; while M. Groute's formidable legal observations pertaining to the ship *Flora,* eight pages long, with a covering letter, are in the Franklin Papers, Historical Society of Pennsylvania, also in Philadelphia.

Apart from Franklinania, one of the most profitable sources for material relative to his privateers turned up in the Admiralty files in the Public Records Office, London. It was a little bundle of papers labeled, "Letters from Sundrys giving inform[n] of the piratical Vessel Black Prince." It proved a veritable gold mine, containing information about the privateer made by former prisoners in her, an attested copy of Marchant's American commission countersigned by Franklin, a copy of a ransom bill, and numerous letters telling of her depredations. These papers are identified as Admiralty I, Secretary In-Letters, Intelligence, Ser 2d, Vol. 3973, 412–449. Another item from the Admiralty files, and identified as Secretary In-Letters, Vol. 1790, was a letter from Captain George Farmer, of His Majesty's ship *Quebec,* telling how he recaptured six prizes taken by the *Black Prince* during her first cruise.

Other occasional printed or manuscript sources are given in the footnotes.

# Index

Aberdeen, Scotland, 158
Adams, John, 77, 138
*Alarm*, British cutter, 115 n.
*Alligator*, British privateer brig, 134
*Alliance*, American frigate, 19, 171
American Commissioners to France, 9, 17 n.; approve French prize regulations, 77
American commissions, 14, 15; Ryan's desire for, 7, 24; Marchant's requests for, 16, 19; Franklin asks need for, 17, 76; De Clonard's interest in, 19, 20; Coffyn's recommendations for, 20, 25, 62, 63; issuance of, 21, 95, 100, 121; conspiracy to secure, 23–26; Torris' applications for, 78, 120, 121; Coffyn explains need for, 93, 94; reasons for granting of, explained to Vergennes, 140–42; withdrawal of, 164–67, 170, 172; Franklin's recollections of use of, 175
American Legation Letter Books, 17 n.
American Navy, vi, 11, 12, 14, 18
*American Neptune,* 109 n.
American Philosophical Society, vi, 10 n.
American privateers, *see* Privateers, American
*American Privateers at Dunkerque,* 102 n., 166 n., 175 n.
American Revolution, 17, 18
American Tories, 76
Amsterdam, 34, 67

*Ann,* British brig, ransomed by *Black Prince,* 46; sea paroles given crew of, 47; arrival of, at Penzance, 52
Ardmore Head, Ireland, 69
*A Relic of the Revolution,* 18 n.
*Ariel,* American frigate, 158 n.
Arnold, Lieutenant Jonathan, 21, 27, 49, 102 n.; capture of, 55, 67
Armed neutrality, 138
Audierne, Brittany, 108
*Aurora,* British frigate, 115 n., 156 n.
Azores (Western Islands), 68

Baltic Sea, 106, 148, 150, 158; British fleet in, scattered by Jones, 97
Barclay, Thomas, 32 n.
Bardsley Island, 148
Barmouth, Wales, 7, 107
Barra Head, Hebrides, 126, 127
Barry, Wales, 68
Bas, Isle of, 38, 67, 109, 135, 155
Basset's Cove (Portreath), Cornwall, 46, 68
Baudouin, Chevalier de, 30, 31
Beachy Head, Sussex, 35
Belfast, Ireland, 6, 85, 86
Bell, John, master, British ship *Hopewell,* 84
Bennett, Richard, alias for Macatter, 5
Berck, France, 129, 130, 132, 142
Bergen, Norway, 126
Bernardson, Peter, 26
*Besborough,* British mail packet,